1⬤1 MUST PLACES TO VISIT IN KENTUCKY BEFORE YOU DIE

GARY P. WEST

Acclaim Press™
MORLEY, MISSOURI

Acclaim Press
— *Your Next Great Book* —

P.O. Box 238
Morley, MO 63767
(573) 472-9800
www.acclaimpress.com

Book Design by:

G R A P H I C   D E S I G N

Designer: Mary Ellen Sikes
Cover Design: M. Frene Melton

ISBN-13: 978-1-935001-29-4
ISBN-10: 1-935001-29-9
Library of Congress Catalog No.: 2009909418

Printed in the United States of America
First Printing: 2009
10 9 8 7 6 5 4 3 2 1

Additional copies may be purchased from Acclaim Press.

This publication was produced using available information. The Publisher regrets it cannot assume responsibility for errors or omissions.

Cover Postcards courtesy of Ray Buckberry.

Contents

Dedication

To Deborah, my wife, who has waded through five of my books and numerous magazine and newspaper articles, successfully transferring my virtually unreadable longhand into somthing my publisher could turn into a book.

Foreword

Many years ago, my father and I made a trip west to the Land Between the Lakes from our home in Barren County in south central Kentucky. It was a rare vacation for both of us. Dad was devoted to his business in Glasgow and didn't get too far away from his customers in those days. This was a glorious exception. I still remember the long-legged egrets feeding on the river bank, barges as big as our house, a horseback ride through the forest. I particularly cherished the trip because we had left my two sisters at home; this adventure was just for Dad and me.

Recently, I traveled back to Lake Barkley. This trip reminded me of how much the lake region has to offer visitors from around the state, and around the world. I also had a chance to detour to Fancy Farm, for the picnic and political speeches that take place there the first Saturday in August for well over a hundred years. It is the one political event that no aspiring statewide office-holder wants to miss, and you shouldn't miss it either.

Fancy Farm and the Land Between the Lakes are just two of the many wonderful, you-can't-afford-to-miss places and events that you will discover, or re-discover, as you read this engaging book.

In *101 Must Places to Visit*, Gary West, who also wrote *Eating Your Way Across Kentucky* and *Shopping Your Way Across Kentucky*, has captured enough localities to keep your travel schedule booked for years. There is probably no other writer in the state who has written more about the fascinating people, places and things you find in the Bluegrass state.

And, this compilation will not disappoint. From A for Abraham Lincoln's birthplace near Hodgenville to Z for the Zachary Taylor Cemetery in Louisville, Gary will entertain and delight you with his knowledge and mesmerizing detail that will force you into your automobile for a cross-state adventure you'll never forget. The tales you'll tell about the discoveries you find. I can't count the number of times my wife and I have told our story of staying overnight at the Wigwam Village in Cave City. I had grown up in the same county where the teepees stand, and driven past them for years!

Suggestion: Don't drive past any of these intriguing Kentucky landmarks. Instead, make them a destination.

I have fond memories of the time when dad and I made that trip to LBL. Since then, I've had many opportunities to visit a special place, a historic sight, or a scenic view I've wanted to share with him. Be sure you take Gary West's guide with you the next time you decide to travel Kentucky and introduce yourself, your friends and family to the many wonders this state has to offer.

Bill Goodman
Producer/host of *Kentucky Tonight, One to One and bookclub@ket*

Introduction

Over the past several years some of my friends have said they would like to do what I'm doing: writing books about interesting places to eat and fun places to shop. I've replied with the much overused phrase, but appropriate, that "somebody had to do it."

Criss-crossing the state, visiting almost all of Kentucky's 120 counties, the sometime unexpected beauty would jump out and slap me right in the face.

In these pages I have assembled *101 Must Places To Visit in Kentucky Before You Die*. Some might consider it a collection or assortment, while others might even refer to these sites as a hodgepodge. It really doesn't matter.

What matters is that many of these "Must Places" are probably just down the road from where you live. Some are well-known attractions, others not so much. Some cost to see, while some are free. Regardless, all are worth a visit.

When putting together a book that basically is a list, I run the risk of leaving something or someplace out. That goes with the territory.

A book listing 101 must places to visit is a huge undertaking. However, in the end it confirms an inventory of some of the best-known and unknown places in Kentucky.

One thing I've learned from visiting these venues is that five different people can visit the same site and come away with five different reactions. For sure none of us like or enjoy the same things.

You can be sure that in these pages there is something for everyone. Some are historical, some entertaining, others outright fun, while a few are whimsical or even quirky.

For the convenience of travelers, this book is broken down into five different regions. It's evident that there is a concentration of "must places" in and around the larger towns throughout Kentucky, with more in Louisville and Lexington. Because of this, I have included a separate section on these two cities, making it easier to visit more in a shorter period of time. But in no way should you let this deter you from hitting the back roads of this beautiful state and seeing some incredible things.

For several years now, Kentucky has been on the Unbridled Spirit marketing kick. I like it. I like it because to me it denotes a certain amount of inquisitiveness, much the same that surely Dr. Thomas Walker and Daniel Boone must have had in 1750 when they came through Cumberland Gap into Kentucky.

It's that spirit that urges us to march on. When others think they have gone far enough, Kentuckians want to know what lies ahead.

What's over the next hill? What's around the next curve?

Every Kentucky county is beautiful. Each one has a story to tell and places to see. Because of this, it was not easy deciding what 101 places to include in the book. The exclusion of any place or places is in no way a reflection of its non-worthiness. The truth is if I were listing 201 must places, I would still be faced with the same dilemma. Indeed, there are hundreds of wonderful places to visit in Kentucky.

There are so many places to see and visit in beautiful Kentucky that it doesn't seem fair to all of those not mentioned.

A book like this is only intended to get you going. There's a good chance you will be exposed to other wonderful places and sites, even while in route to something in these pages.

Bill Monroe Homeplace	Rosine, Ky
Columbus-Belmont State Park	Columbus, Ky
Fancy Farm Picnic	Fancy Farm, Ky
John James Audubon State Park	Henderson, Ky
Kentucky Lake	Western Ky
Land Between the Lakes	Golden Pond, Ky
Museum of Fine Art	Owensboro, Ky
National Quilt Museum	Paducah, Ky
Riverside Park	Dawson Springs, Ky
The Strange Procession That Never Moves	Mayfield, Ky

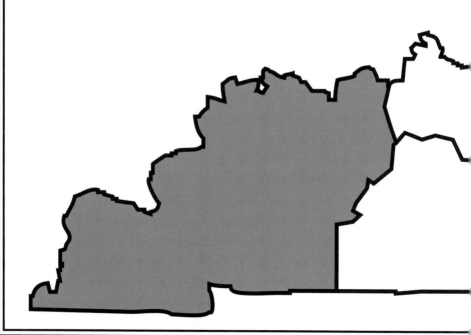

Western Region

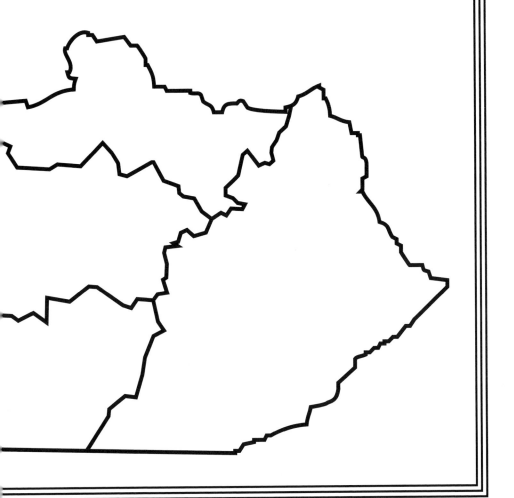

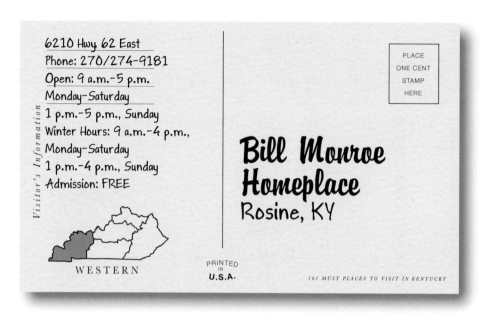

6210 Hwy 62 East
Phone: 270/274-9181
Open: 9 a.m.-5 p.m.
Monday-Saturday
1 p.m.-5 p.m., Sunday
Winter Hours: 9 a.m.-4 p.m.,
Monday-Saturday
1 p.m.-4 p.m., Sunday
Admission: FREE

Visitor's Information

PLACE
ONE CENT
STAMP
HERE

**Bill Monroe
Homeplace**
Rosine, KY

WESTERN

PRINTED
IN
U.S.A.

101 MUST PLACES TO VISIT IN KENTUCKY

Bluegrass music fans consider a visit to Jerusalem Ridge, and Bill Monroe's old Homeplace that sits nearby, a pilgrimage.

Monroe was born September 13, 1911, just outside of Rosine in Ohio County, and the Homeplace today sits on five of the farm's original 1,000 acres. Restored in 2001, it is now a shrine to the Monroe family and the music they played.

It was Monroe and his Blue Grass Boys who strolled onto the Grand Ole Opry stage in 1939, captivated the audience and then the world

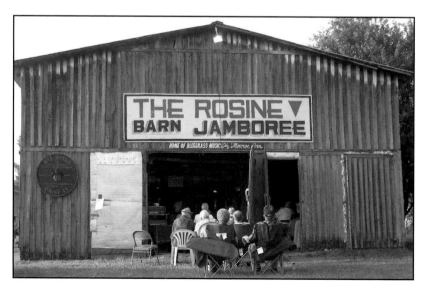

with a new kind of music. That performance led to a cult-like following that soon had a nation clamoring to see and hear him play. If that was not possible, listeners tuned their box-style radios to Nashville's WSM and the Opry each Saturday night.

Called the "Father of Bluegrass Music," Monroe became a legend with his unusual style and one-of-a-kind technique. He played his mandolin and produced a sound not heard before, and today he remains the only person ever to be inducted into three Halls of Fame – Bluegrass, Country, and Rock and Roll. To add credence to how famous he had become, in 1995 President Clinton presented Monroe with the National Medal of the Arts.

Monroe died in 1996, but his music lives on and his Homeplace is quite popular.

Family photos and musical instruments are there, but it's the tour guides who bring it all to life. They spin their stories from a first-hand account, as most knew Monroe or grew up just across the ridge from him.

Just down the road is the Rosine Barn Jamboree. A stage here gives locals a forum to carry on the legacy. Fiddles, mandolins, guitars and banjos are usually the musical instruments of choice here.

350 Park Road
Phone: 270/677-2327

PLACE
ONE CENT
STAMP
HERE

Visitor's Information

Columbus-Belmont State Park
Columbus, KY

WESTERN

PRINTED
IN
U.S.A.

101 MUST PLACES TO VISIT IN KENTUCKY

Because of its location in far western Kentucky, near where the Ohio River flows into the mighty Mississippi, Columbus was considered important territory during the Civil War.

But because of its location in far western Kentucky, it's a safe bet that few Kentuckians have visited this strategic site that was once used to control what river traffic went up and down the Mississippi River.

With as many as 19,000 Confederate soldiers occupying Columbus, the site overlooking the river became known as the "Gibraltar of the West." With gunboats patrolling the river, heavy guns positioned on bluffs from above, the Confederates still stretched a gigantic mile-long chain of 20-pound links across the river. The chain was supported by stationary barges in the river, and firmly secured by a buried six-ton ocean anchor and attached to the bank on the Columbus side. On the Missouri side of Belmont the chain was equally secured.

After several failed attempts by Union forces to

16

take Columbus, the Confederate positions were finally vacated when on March 1 and 2 of 1862, they were outflanked and outmaneuvered. With them they took their supplies, ammo, heavy guns and gun crews to another position down river.

Today visitors can visit Columbus-Belmont State Park. Remnant earthwork fortifications can be seen, along with the largest Civil War cannon in Kentucky. The cannon weighs 7,545 pounds. It took a big gun to fire a 32-pounder.

The six-ton anchor with several feet of the huge chain still attached, is prominently displayed at the park that overlooks the Mississippi River and beyond into Missouri.

Columbus is a small town of less than 300 residents, and history documents its significance during the Civil War, but it was said that long before then during the presidency of Thomas Jefferson, a Washington, D.C. fire caused Jefferson to propose that the U.S. capital be moved to the centrally-located town of Columbus, Kentucky. His proposal is said to have failed in the Senate by one vote.

Another foot note is that at the age of 15, legendary railroader Casey Jones got his first job as a telegrapher for the Mobile & Ohio Railroad here.

17

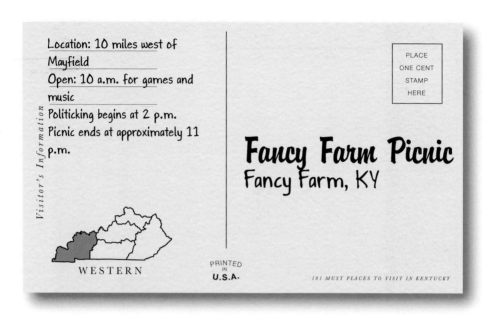

Location: 10 miles west of Mayfield

Open: 10 a.m. for games and music

Politicking begins at 2 p.m.

Picnic ends at approximately 11 p.m.

PLACE
ONE CENT
STAMP
HERE

Fancy Farm Picnic
Fancy Farm, KY

WESTERN

PRINTED
IN
U.S.A.

101 MUST PLACES TO VISIT IN KENTUCKY

O n the surface, Fancy Farm in Graves County in western Kentucky is a sleepy little village anchored by the St. Jerome Catholic Church.

For 364 days out of the year, that's what it is. But on the first Saturday of every August, Fancy Farm turns into the Incredible Hulk.

That's when some 15,000 people including dozens of politicians looking for votes, converge on Fancy Farm for what is advertised as the "World's Largest One Day Picnic."

Since 1880, people have been gathering here for a good time. As the years have gone by, the event has turned into the unofficial kick-off of fall campaigning in Kentucky politics.

The day is a throwback to when candidates sought out an elevated old tree stump, where they would proceed to give a rousing speech that often brought out hurrahs or good natured boos.

This longtime tradition has died in

many states, but at Fancy Farm it has been kept alive. A place to see and be seen in political circles, this event is sponsored by the St. Jerome Catholic Church.

Its carnival-like-atmosphere includes games, bluegrass and country music, and food, lots of it. In fact each year about 18,000 pounds of barbeque pork and mutton, 1,400 pounds of chicken, hamburgers, hot dogs, 400 pounds each of potato salad and coleslaw, and pies and cakes are served. This is unique in that the "picnic" is entirely a community effort with no outside vendors, and takes place on the grounds of Fancy Farm elementary school.

For years, political oratory took place under a large oak tree, but in 1974 lightning struck and killed the tree, causing Kentucky Governor Louie Nunn to say, "Too much fertilizer will kill anything."

Although statewide candidates are the norm, the event over the years has attracted the likes of Texas Senator Lloyd Bentsen, George Wallace, Al Gore, Alben Barkley and Happy Chandler. Chandler made his first appearance in 1931.

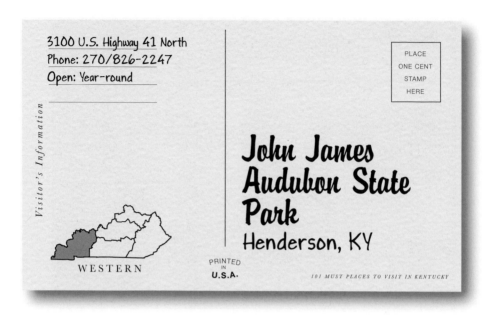

3100 U.S. Highway 41 North
Phone: 270/826-2247
Open: Year-round

Visitor's Information

John James Audubon State Park
Henderson, KY

WESTERN

PRINTED
IN
U.S.A.

101 MUST PLACES TO VISIT IN KENTUCKY

This more than 700 acre state park in western Kentucky pays tribute to one of the world's most recognizable bird and wildlife artist, John James Audubon.

Audubon, who was actually born in Haiti, lived in Henderson from 1810 to 1819. Here, he operated several small businesses with mixed success. Without question it was his interest in the outdoors that led to his drawings and paintings of wildlife and birds.

His paintings became well known throughout England and Scotland, and he had achieved modest acclaim in America. Audubon's life

story shows how a passion and dedication to accomplish something can overcome many of life's adversities. He died at the age of 65 and is buried in the Trinity Cemetery in New York City.

Today at the state park named in his honor, visitors can see the Museum and Nature Center that presents an interpretation of Audubon's life through his paintings, sketches, and personal memorabilia.

The Nature Center is made up of three different areas: a wildlife observation room, the discovery room, which offers several hands-on exhibits; and the learning room, where the park naturalist and arts educator combine for a program.

The State Park offers a variety of year-round interpretive programs under a well-trained park staff, with a focus on art history, native plants, animals, conservation, and even recycling.

Six rental cottages, campgrounds, and hiking trail make this a fun place to walk the same grounds that John James Audubon did almost 200 years ago. And you won't be disappointed with the first rate gift shop. From Audubon reproduction prints, that include songbirds, birds of prey, and the ivory-billed woodpecker, to books on birding, bird houses, feeders and garden art, this shop is an "outdoorsy" delight.

Kentucky Dam Village State Resort
Park, 800/325-0146
Kentucky State Resort Park,
800/325-0143
Lake Barkley State Resort Park,
800/325-1708
Marshall County Tourism,
800/467-7145

Visitor's Information

PLACE
ONE CENT
STAMP
HERE

Kentucky Lake
Western Kentucky

WESTERN

PRINTED
IN
U.S.A.

101 MUST PLACES TO VISIT IN KENTUCKY

Kentucky Lake is the second largest man-made lake in the United States, covering 2,380 miles of shoreline and 160,000 acres of water.

This is one great recreational lake.

With fish, wildlife and boating, outdoor recreational activities is a mainstay of this western Kentucky attraction.

An estimated four million visitors a year from throughout the United States come to the area, and as might be expected there is an abundance of private rental cabins, cottages, and, not one, but three, Kentucky State Park resorts with lodging and nearby marinas.

Kentucky Dam Village State Resort Park features the largest marina in the park system. Other area parks are Kenlake State Resort Park and Lake Barkley State Resort Park.

Because of the size of Kentucky Lake one of the big selling points to boaters is they can enjoy water skiing, fishing, cruising, and house boating in a relatively uncrowded setting.

Something unique to Kentucky Lake is that boats from other parts of the country can actually travel in and out by connecting waterways that flow into the Mississippi and Ohio Rivers. On a given day some sizable yachts, sailboats and houseboats can be seen docked at one of the marinas or slowly cruising the lake and taking in some of the beautiful shore line scenery.

2995 Lincoln Farm Road

Phone: 270/924-2000 or

800/LBL-7077

Open: Year-round

Admission: FREE

Visitor's Information

PLACE
ONE CENT
STAMP
HERE

Land Between
the Lakes
Golden Pond, KY

WESTERN

PRINTED
IN
U.S.A.

101 MUST PLACES TO VISIT IN KENTUCKY

Land Between the Lakes (LBL) is an area, not one specific thing. It's a national recreation area located in the western part of Kentucky and Tennessee.

Managed by the United States Forest Service, this 170,000-acre reserve has some 300 miles of undeveloped shoreline on both Kentucky Lake and Lake Barkley. Both lakes can claim it because, this parcel of land sits between both.

As an area, LBL is one of Kentucky's most popular tourist attractions, with Lake Barkley State Resort Park sitting just across the lake on

the Cumberland River side, and Kentucky Lake State Resort Park on the Tennessee River side. It received its national designation by President John F. Kennedy in 1963.

The area offers a broad range of outdoor opportunities from environmental education, to historic interpretation, that even includes the role the area played during the Civil War.

A Visitors Center at Golden Pond just off Hwy. 68/80 features an observatory and planetarium.

In the planetarium, beginner astronomers can learn about ways to identify the constellations in a simulated night sky. And in the observatory stars can be observed through one of the four telescopes.

LBL also features a 700-acre Elk and Bison Prairie with designated viewing areas.

The Home Place is a living history farm from the 1850s, complete with on-site docents duplicating farm life in period dress and period agricultural techniques.

Many Land Between the Lakes activities are seasonal, so be sure and call ahead for schedules.

Museum of Fine Art

Owensboro, KY

There's something about a visit to the Museum of Fine Art in Owensboro that just makes you feel better. It's one of those wonderful museums that offer up a pleasant surprise of sophistication and culture, while at the same time a certain amount reflects the southern heritage that includes Kentucky art from as far back as the early 1800s.

The art collection here is diverse, to say the least. American, European and Asian exhibits are among the treasures of international works. Among them: French Impressionist Master, Edgar Degas (1834-1917), English portraitist, Sir Thomas Lawrence (1769-1839), American painters Martin Johnson Heade (1819-1904), Charles Willson Peale (1741-1827), and Frank Duveneck (1848-1919).

American contemporary artists displaying are the likes of Joe Downing, Jack Youngman, Robert Berks, T.D. Kelsey, Peter Reginato, and Harry Jackson.

Perhaps the marquee feature of the museum is the Stained Glass Gallery. This not-easy-to-forget exhibit consist of 16 turn-of-the-century stained glass windows permanently installed in 25-foot towers crafted by internationally acclaimed German-American glass maker Emil Frei (1867-1941).

The museum consists of three wings that feature 15 temporary and permanent galleries, plus a house museum in a pre-Civil War era structure. Complementing it all are two outdoor sculpture parks.

Although Owensboro is one of the larger cities in Kentucky, a museum of this caliber usually would be found in much larger places.

Located downtown, the Museum of Fine Art puts quite a bit of effort in bringing in "outside" collections that allow visitors to experience rare visual arts from around the world.

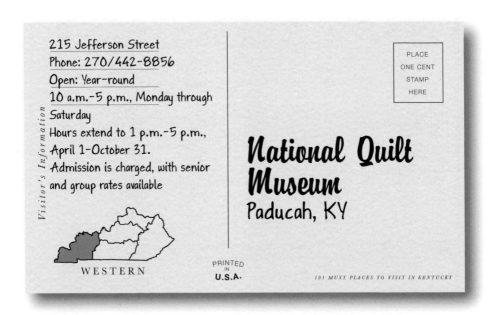

215 Jefferson Street
Phone: 270/442-8856
Open: Year-round
10 a.m.-5 p.m., Monday through
Saturday
Hours extend to 1 p.m.-5 p.m.,
April 1-October 31.
Admission is charged, with senior
and group rates available

Visitor's Information

WESTERN

National Quilt Museum

Paducah, KY

PRINTED
IN
U.S.A.

101 MUST PLACES TO VISIT IN KENTUCKY

I t's the largest quilt museum in the world, and this Paducah attraction is now designated as The National Quilt Museum of the United States.

The Museum has more than 150 quilts on exhibit, with a continuous transition of quilt displays rotating in and out in order to keep it fresh for visitors who come back again and again.

Gallery Talks by the actual quilters are often a part of the traveling exhibits.

Stained glass windows based on specific quilts grace the lobby, and visitors also get the opportunity to see a beautiful hand-carved wooden quilt hanging in the Conference Room.

The Quilt Museum was opened in April 1991, after being funded and built by Bill and Meredith Schroeder from Paducah. The two had become interested in the art form of quilting in 1983. They had become so impressed with the extraordinary work being created, that they wanted to establish something that would recognize those involved for years to come. And they did, with this beautiful facility in downtown Paducah.

The styles of quilt making are often as varied as the assortment of colors used to make them, and the Museum prides itself in exhibiting both contemporary and traditional works.

The Museum, under the direction of the Museum of the American Quilters Society, has become a major attraction, drawing visitors from throughout the world. Guided tours are free to groups scheduled in advance. Tour lengths range from a 15-minute introduction, to an in-depth tour of 40 minutes.

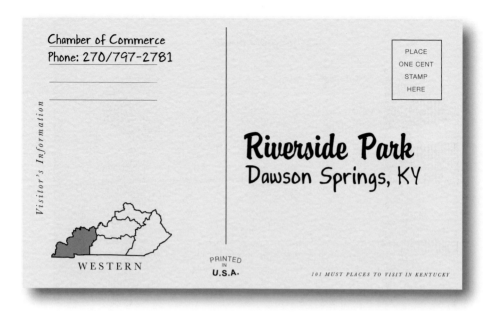

PLACE
ONE CENT
STAMP
HERE

Visitor's Information

Riverside Park
Dawson Springs, KY

WESTERN

PRINTED
IN
U.S.A.

101 MUST PLACES TO VISIT IN KENTUCKY

Riverside Baseball Park is more about its history than anything else. It's the history of this old park and the town's three years of baseball glory when it hosted the Pittsburgh Pirates from 1914 through 1916 for their annual spring training.

Back then big league teams in the east didn't travel to the deep south for spring training like they do today. Rail lines weren't developed in that area of the country. They did, however, pass through Dawson Springs.

For years the town had been recognized for its abundance of natural mineral springs, of which many thought had cure-all health benefits.

At one time Dawson Springs had 41 hotels and boarding houses, and although its winter population was 1,500, once spring and summer arrived it ballooned to 15,000.

In 1914, the Pittsburgh Pirates and their legendary shortstop Honus Wagner

arrived. Almost a century later folks are still talking about it.

One of the things that keep the history alive is that the old ball park is still there today, and what makes it even more special is that baseball games are still being played there.

A summer college team, called the Tradewater Pirates, participates at the hallowed site, where some of the greatest to ever play the game once took their turn in the batter's box.

Riverside Park sits in a sharp bend of the Tradewater, an 80 mile river that flows into the Ohio. Today, families flock to the park during the summer, picnicking or enjoying what some visitors claim is the best ballpark food in the country.

The old bones of the park are quite evident, and it's fun to imagine what it was like when old Honus strolled to the plate. One of the greatest of all-time, he walked the streets of Dawson Springs and patrolled the infield at Riverside Park. A .329 lifetime batting average, eight National League batting titles, and 17 consecutive years of batting .300 or better, proves the point.

This is a fun experience, especially for a baseball fan, to visit here. Located in Hopkins County, not far from Madisonville, it's easy to get to just off the Western Kentucky Parkway at Exit 24.

Maplewood Cemetery
Hwy 121 and Housman Street East
Phone: 270/247-6101
Website: www.mayfieldchamber.com

PLACE
ONE CENT
STAMP
HERE

Visitor's Information

The Strange Procession That Never Moves
Mayfield, KY

WESTERN

PRINTED
IN
U.S.A.

101 MUST PLACES TO VISIT IN KENTUCKY

You may travel throughout the world and visit thousands of cemeteries, but in all probability you will not see anything like the Wooldridge Monuments in Maplewood Cemetery in Mayfield.

The oddity of these sixteen statues lined up as if ready to move forward in a small-town parade, is totally out of the norm. And it has remained that way since Henry Wooldridge began commissioning the figures to be placed on a sixteen-by-thirty plot in the cemetery well before his death in 1899.

Wooldridge, who went by the name of Colonel, made his living buying and selling horses. Considered a man of means, and never marrying, his later years in life revolved around creating this unorthodox collection of people and animals.

The statues are so unusual that they have been written about in *Ripley's Believe It or Not*, photographed by Walker Evans in 1947, used as a backdrop in the movie *In Country*, and even alluded to in a William Faulkner story.

Colonel Wooldridge initially paid $1,000 to have a statute of himself sculptured from marble in Italy. The remaining 15 were done in Paducah and Mayfield.

To make it even a little more strange, Wooldridge is the only one buried here. His entourage includes his widowed mother, three brothers, three sisters, two nieces, his two dogs, a fox and a deer.

Just to make this graveyard scene even more difficult to understand,

32

Colonel Wooldridge has two statues of himself, one is his younger days standing tall, and the other sitting stately on his fifteen-hand high horse, Fop.

It is reported that $6,000 was spent on all of the sculptures, and that the Colonel intended to have more carved, but died before he could.

William Lydon, a sculptor from Paducah carved twelve of the sixteen statues. When completed they were transported on flatbed rail cars to Mayfield.

Abraham Lincoln Birthplace	Hodgenville, Ky
Beaumont Inn	Harrodsburg, Ky
Bernheim Forest	Clermont, Ky
Bourbon Trail	Six Counties
Center for Kentucky History	Frankfort, Ky
Constitution Square	Danville, Ky
Federal Hill	Bardstown, Ky
Frankfort Cemetery	Frankfort, Ky
Gold Vault	Ft. Knox, Ky
Governor's Mansion	Frankfort, Ky
Great American Dollhouse Museum	Danville, Ky
Kentucky State Capitol	Frankfort, Ky
Kentucky Vietnam Veterans Memorial	Frankfort, Ky
Lincoln Jamboree	Hodgenville, Ky
Lower Howard's Creek	Winchester, Ky
My Old Kentucky Dinner Train	Bardstown, Ky
Old State Capitol	Frankfort, Ky
Patton Museum	Ft. Knox, Ky
Perryville Battlefield	Perryville, Ky
Renfro Valley	Mt. Vernon, Ky
Schmidt Museum of Coca-Cola	Elizabethtown, Ky

Central Region

Shaker Village of Pleasant Hill	Harrodsburg, Ky
Somernite Cruise	Somerset, Ky
Great American Brass Band Festival	Danville, Ky
Toyota Plant Tour	Georgetown, Ky
White Hall	Richmond, Ky
Winery Tours	Kentucky
World's Longest Yard Sale	Hwy 127
Yew Dell Gardens	Crestwood, Ky

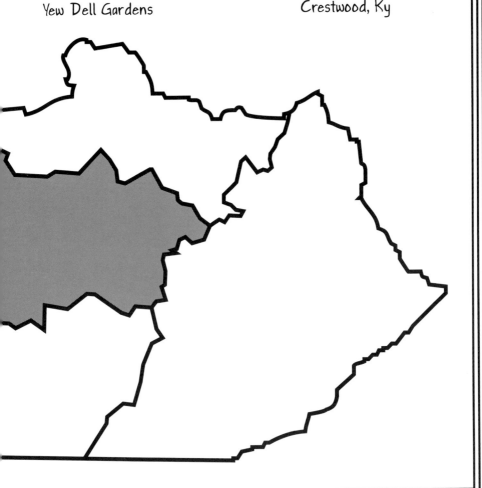

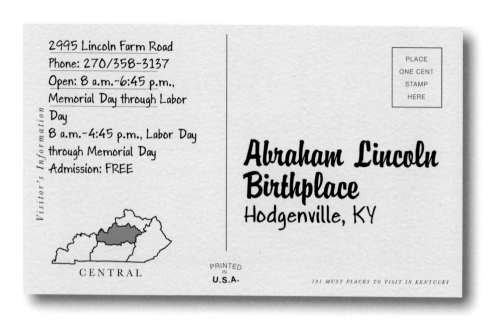

2995 Lincoln Farm Road
Phone: 270/358-3137
Open: 8 a.m.-6:45 p.m.,
Memorial Day through Labor
Day
8 a.m.-4:45 p.m., Labor Day
through Memorial Day
Admission: FREE

Visitor's Information

CENTRAL

PRINTED
IN
U.S.A.

Abraham Lincoln Birthplace
Hodgenville, KY

101 MUST PLACES TO VISIT IN KENTUCKY

Whether it's the actual cabin of our sixteenth President of the United States, or pieces from it, makes little difference, because the grounds are hallowed.

Abraham Lincoln's parents, Thomas and Nancy settled on what was called Sinking Spring Farm in 1808, and two months later on February

12, 1809, he was born in a one-room log cabin. The so-called symbolic one is displayed inside the impressive granite and marble structure. This temple-like building fronted by six huge columns with 56 steps leading up to the cabin, was built between 1909-1911 by the Lincoln Farm Association and deeded to the U.S. government on Labor Day 1916, when President Woodrow Wilson was on hand to accept it. That same year the grounds became a National Park.

The Lincoln Farm consists of 116-acres, and although grounds are quite impressive, it's the cabin that is the big draw.

The logs of the reconstructed cabin, some oak, some chestnut, are believed to be of the period. For sure it is a snapshot of Lincoln's humble beginnings. The one-room structure measures 13 x 17 feet and has one door, a single window, fireplace and dirt floor.

Other U.S. Presidents preceded Wilson's visit to the grounds. Teddy Roosevelt addressed a crowd when the cornerstone was placed on February 12, 1909, for the construction of the memorial building. And then President William Howard Taft was on hand when the building was completed on November 9, 1911.

A nearby reception center displays several Lincoln family artifacts of interest as well as a short film depicting Abraham Lincoln's childhood in Kentucky.

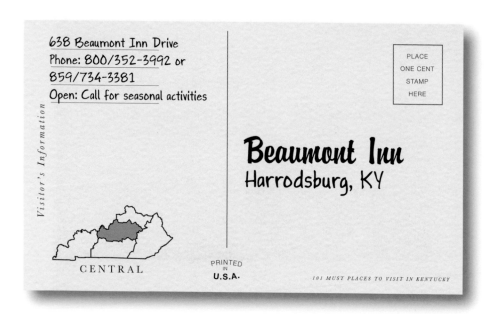

PLACE
ONE CENT
STAMP
HERE

Visitor's Information

Beaumont Inn
Harrodsburg, KY

CENTRAL

PRINTED
IN
U.S.A.

101 MUST PLACES TO VISIT IN KENTUCKY

Constructed in 1845 as a school for young ladies, today the Beaumont Inn reeks with genuine hospitality, just as it did years ago.

Upon entering the tree dotted landscape, the 30-acre grounds are a welcoming site, letting visitors know immediately that this is a special place.

The well-appointed main inn was formerly a girl's college, but since 1919 it has been operated by the Dedman family as a first class fine country inn.

It features a dining room that serves a traditional southern cuisine, the likes of which will make you come back again and again. In fact it has been so good for so many years that it was travel guru Duncan Hines' favorite place to eat in all of Kentucky.

Today the Beaumont Inn is operated by Chuck and Helen Dedman, and son Dixon.

You don't need many reasons to visit this comfortable place. But in case you do: lodging, dining, or shopping in their wonderful gift shop that features many one-of-a-kind items, all combine for a most relaxing experience.

Antiques, and family memorabilia, as well as pictures of days gone by when Beaumont was a college, are entertaining and educational ways to spend some time. Or you can settle in one of the over-sized chairs in one of the inn's two parlors and read a book.

Outside, visitors can stroll the half-mile walking path, enjoying the 37 species of trees, flowers and birds.

As upscale-casual as the main dining room is, the Old Owl Tavern in the lower level offers a change of pace. Mainly a bar-grub menu, it is totally casual with a full-service bar enhanced by a big wood burning fireplace.

Exit 112 I-65, Ky Highway 245

Phone: 502/955-8512

Open: 7 a.m. to sunset, except Christmas & New Years

Admission: free on weekdays; $5 per vehicle on weekends and holidays

Visitor's Information

Bernheim Forest
Clermont, Ky

CENTRAL

PRINTED IN U.S.A.

101 MUST PLACES TO VISIT IN KENTUCKY

Bernheim Arboretum and Research Forest is a private entity established in 1929 by Isaac Bernheim, a distiller in the area. The land had been stripped by early salt and iron pioneers. Bernheim purchased and replanted the lush park that visitors see today. Various endowments left by Bernheim have ensured the Forest's future.

Just a couple of minutes off I-65 in Bullitt County, Bernheim Forest and its 14,000 acres seem to pop up out of nowhere. With a relatively new Visitors Center, visitors are ensured the opportunity to experience the fullest of this jewel-of-an-experience.

With its 50-miles of hiking and biking trails, and 250-acre official state arboretum, visitors can see more than 2,800 labeled trees and shrubs, a fishing lake and picnic facilities.

Visitors can check out hand-held computers that allow them to become an interactive part of the exhibits in the forest. These devices display the special tags throughout the grounds, and reveal information about native plants and animals in the forest.

The Visitors Center was designed to be environmentally friendly in order to maximize light and heat. Recycled Heinz pickle vats and a wood ceiling made from old Jim Beam bourbon rack houses, make sure the building conforms to the environmental standards at Bernheim.

There are interesting geological formations, historic homesteads, native wildlife, wildflowers and water features with conveniently-placed benches for visitors to enjoy.

Bernheim Forest is one of those destinations that are always in season. Whether in bloom or not this is a place for year-round family fun.

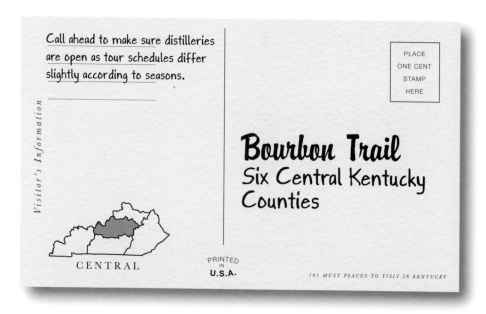

Bourbon Trail
Six Central Kentucky Counties

For years it's been said that Kentucky makes three-fourths of the world's bourbon, and three-fourths of the state's 120 counties are dry.

Kentucky does in fact distill a lot of bourbon. And because of it, bourbon has been a big part of the state's promotional efforts. It's a part of the state's heritage and culture that dates back over 200 years.

Most people don't know the difference between bourbon and whiskey. Some bottles say bourbon and others whiskey.

Why?

Federal regulations stipulate that distillers meet six requirements in order for products to be called bourbon.

First it must be made in America. It must be aged in a new white

oak charred barrel. Corn must be the primary grain, 51% to 79%. It cannot be distilled over 160 proof, and it cannot be entered into the barrel over 125 proof. And finally, no filtering or additives can be used to change the taste or color.

If all six of these steps are not followed everything else is whiskey, not bourbon.

It just so happens that pretty much of Kentucky's distilleries are located in the same proximity of the state, within an hour of each other.

How did this happen?

Some say it's a coincidence. Some say it's the water. Some say it was the accessibility to the oak barrels and nearby grain. Others even say it's the humidity in the aging process.

Perhaps it's a little of each, but the good thing is visitors can now see good ole Kentucky bourbon being made at one or all of the state's seven largest distilleries on "Kentucky's Bourbon Trail."

Perhaps the best place to start the trail is at the Oscar Getz Whiskey Museum (502/348-2999) in Bardstown. Although not a distillery, it does jump start your adventures with a little history.

Heaven Hill, (502/337-1000) Nelson County. Here you'll hear about Evan Williams, Kentucky's first distiller, and Rev. Elijah Craig, the father of bourbon.

- Jim Beam (502/543-9877), Bullitt County. Six generations of Beams.
- Maker's Mark (270/865-2099), Marion County. Visitors can hand-dip their own bottles.
- Four Roses (502/839-3436), Anderson County. Sits on the banks of Salt River since 1911.
- Austin Nichols (502/839-4544), Anderson County. Overlooks the Kentucky River and distills Wild Turkey.
- Labrot & Graham (859/879-1812), Woodford County, Woodford Reserve is the marquee item.
- Buffalo Trace (800/654-8471), Franklin County. Sits on the Kentucky River in Frankfort.
- Tom Moore (502/348-3774) Nelson County. Formerly Barton.

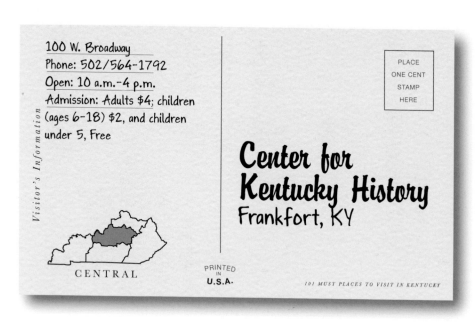

Named in honor of one of the states most well known historians, the Thomas D. Clark Center for Kentucky History, this massive 167,000 square foot building is a must visit when coming to the state's capitol city.

Completed in 1999 at a cost of $29 million, well over a million visitors have toured the facility and retraced Kentucky's history as far back as 12,000 years.

The Center for Kentucky History falls under the umbrella of the Kentucky Historical Society which also oversees the Old State Capitol and Kentucky Military History Museum.

There is so much to see and learn here.

"A Kentucky Journey" is a permanent 20,000 square foot exhibit that gives not only those who live here, but outside visitors a look into where

this state has been and even a hint as to where it's going. The exhibit is laced with hands-on activities as well as interactive exhibits. This is great for children.

All told, museum collections number over 120,000 artifacts, plus more than 8,000 oral history interviews.

The center also houses the Martin F. Schmidt Library that specializes in genealogical research and Kentucky history. Visitor's from throughout the United States use this facility to research family trees as well as history.

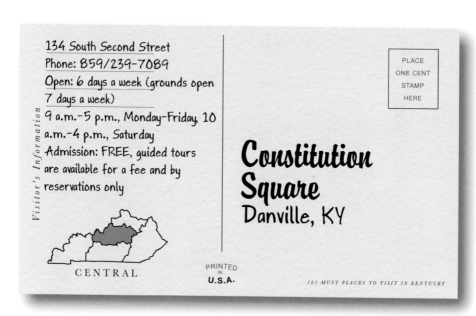

134 South Second Street

Phone: 859/239-7089

Open: 6 days a week (grounds open 7 days a week)

9 a.m.-5 p.m., Monday-Friday, 10 a.m.-4 p.m., Saturday

Admission: FREE, guided tours are available for a fee and by reservations only

Visitor's Information

PLACE
ONE CENT
STAMP
HERE

Constitution Square
Danville, KY

CENTRAL

PRINTED IN U.S.A.

101 MUST PLACES TO VISIT IN KENTUCKY

The birthplace of Kentucky's statehood. What Kentuckian wouldn't want to visit such a place?

While Kentucky was considered a frontier and still a county of Virginia, much effort and years of wading through a difficult process to become the fifteenth state in the Union, was thought to be well worth it. Because of Danville's prominent location in relationship to the Wilderness Road, the town became Kentucky's first governmental location.

Naturally a courthouse had to be built to go along with a meeting house. Over the next several years, from 1784 to 1792, numerous gatherings to discuss a state constitution took place in an effort to separate from Virginia. Finally in April 1792, a state constitution was drafted, and two months later, on June 1, 1792, Kentucky became a state.

Today visitors can see replicas of the courthouse, meetinghouse, jail and other buildings that made up the site of Kentucky's official beginning.

Revolutionary War hero, Isaac Shelby, was named Kentucky's first governor, and as a footnote, he was also the state's fifth governor. He is buried just a few miles south of Danville on U.S. Hwy. 127.

Constitution Square is located in the heart of downtown. It is open year-round. The grounds are open for the public to explore seven days a week, while the visitors' center, gift shop and buildings are open everyday except Sunday.

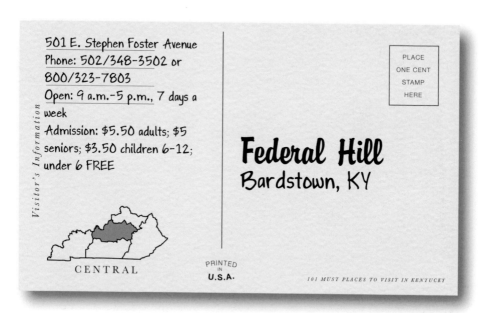

Federal Hill
Bardstown, KY

CENTRAL

PRINTED IN U.S.A.

101 MUST PLACES TO VISIT IN KENTUCKY

I n 1795 Judge John Rowan began to build a house, a Georgian-style home that over time would leave its mark as the inspiration for Kentucky's beloved state song, "My Old Kentucky Home."

Federal Hill, now a State Park, sits on a rise that once overlooked a plantation on the outskirts of Bardstown.

Legend tells the story that Judge Rowan's cousin, Stephen Foster, was inspired to write the song after visiting the site in 1852.

Kentucky's General Assembly, in 1928, made "My Old Kentucky Home" the state's official song.

The backside of the present home was the first phase. Between

1799 and 1802 another portion of the house was added, and then over a ten year period, from 1808 to 1818 the mansions current size was completed.

Federal Hill consists of six rooms open for the tour. Reportedly much of the house was built with slave labor. A freed black woodworker built the intricate windowsills and all of the fireplace mantels throughout the house.

Whether or not Stephen Foster actually visited Federal Hill is not important. Some historians say he did, while others say he did not. What is important is that Kentucky has a beautiful song and an equally beautiful historic home for visitors to tour.

Visitors can also enjoy a nearby amphitheater that features the summer production of "Stephen Foster-The Musical." Begun in 1959, it is the longest continuous outdoor production in the state. The musical features over 50 of Stephen Foster's songs along with singers and actors in colorful period costumes.

The musical combined with a visit to Federal Hill makes for an enjoyable experience.

East Main Street
Phone: 800/960-7200
Open: daylight hours

PLACE
ONE CENT
STAMP
HERE

Visitor's Information

Frankfort
Cemetery
Frankfort, KY

CENTRAL

PRINTED
IN
U.S.A.

101 MUST PLACES TO VISIT IN KENTUCKY

The 100 acre Frankfort Cemetery is one of those places usually not at the top of a tourism list. It is, however, a historical site that once you visit you'll never forget.

Located on East Main Street, the cemetery offers several views of the Kentucky River. A well-appointed stone and iron fence entrance lends stateliness to those arriving. And with the appearance of a beautiful arboretum with its curvy roadway, terraces and numerous vaults, it strikes a sophisticated pose. A central feature to the grounds is the State Mound that highlights a military memorial.

The most famous names here belong to Daniel Boone and wife Rebecca. Seventeen former Kentucky governors are buried here, as are several U.S. senators, politicians, artists, judges and soldiers. A Confederate Monument also occupies space here.

Initially the property consisted of 32 acres and was purchased in 1845 for $3,801. Additional land was purchased in 1858, and then again in 1911.

The cemetery was created by Judge Mason Brown, after an inspirational visit to Mount Auburn Cemetery in Boston. Scottish-born landscape architect Robert Carmichael designed the cemetery, and through his skills was able to take advantage of the rolling topography, meandering river, and bluff overlooking the river offering up views of downtown Frankfort and the Capitol District.

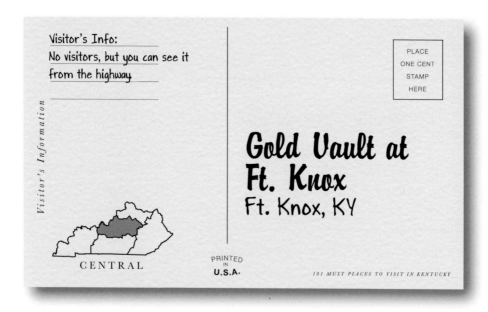

Visitor's Info:
No visitors, but you can see it
from the highway

PLACE
ONE CENT
STAMP
HERE

Visitor's Information

Gold Vault at
Ft. Knox
Ft. Knox, KY

CENTRAL

PRINTED
IN
U.S.A.

101 MUST PLACES TO VISIT IN KENTUCKY

Officially known as the United States Bullion Depository, it is one of those places you can't actually visit, but then again you can.

Visitors can't actually go inside the Gold Vault, but they can at least drive by and see where between $60 billion and $100 billion in solid gold is stacked in the lower level.

With this said it's easy to see why the United States Treasury keeps a tight lid on its security system.

This fortress-like structure surrounds the vault, lined with granite walls and protected by a blast proof door. The combination to the vault is not entrusted to one individual, but instead to several staff members who dial in their portion of the combination, known only to them.

The grounds are surrounded by three fences, supposedly electrified. Armed guards are stationed in bunker-like positions at each corner of the structure. And the truth of the matter is they are authorized to use deadly force if necessary.

The actual building was constructed in 1936, at a cost of $560,000, and ever since it has been engulfed in more legend, mystery and myth than perhaps any other building in America.

These facts are known: the actual structure visitors can see from the roadway is 42-feet high, 121-feet wide, and the vault door in the lower level is 21-inches thick and weighs over 20 tons.

Perhaps nothing drew more attention to Ft. Knox and the Gold Vault than the 1964 James Bond film *Goldfinger*. You can be sure that none of the movie's scenes were shot inside the Gold Vault, and any information about its inner workings was conjured up by Hollywood.

Today a model of the Gold Vault that was used in the film is on display in the Patton Museum at Ft. Knox.

Even as security conscious as the Gold Vault is, it is reported to be the third most photographed building in America behind the U.S. Capital and the White House.

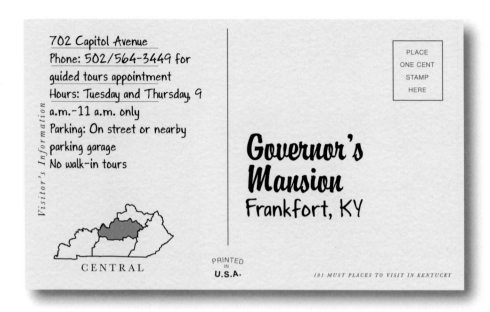

702 Capitol Avenue
Phone: 502/564-3449 for
guided tours appointment
Hours: Tuesday and Thursday, 9
a.m.–11 a.m. only
Parking: On street or nearby
parking garage
No walk-in tours

Visitor's Information

PLACE
ONE CENT
STAMP
HERE

Governor's Mansion
Frankfort, KY

CENTRAL

PRINTED
IN
U.S.A.

101 MUST PLACES TO VISIT IN KENTUCKY

The Governor's Mansion sits on the east lawn of the State Capitol grounds making it convenient for Kentucky's governor to make the leisure stroll from home to office.

The mansion is a thing of elegance and beauty, and the guided tours that are available to the general public bring to the forefront that this home is indeed there for Kentuckians to see and enjoy.

It was designed by C.C. and E.A. Weber from Ft. Thomas, Kentucky in 1912, with the exterior being modeled after the Petit Trianon,

Queen Marie Antoinette's villa near the Palace of Versailles in France.

The structure reflects the grand spirit of people living in the post Civil War's gilded age.

It is quite evident that great care went into the design with attention to exquisite decorative details and the craftsmanship that went with it.

The elegant front portico includes four pairs of Ionic columns, proportioned perfectly with a stone balustrade and terrace that make for a stunning entrance to the home.

Twenty-four governors have lived in the mansion. For a four year period, 1980-1984, the Governor's Mansion underwent an extensive renovation that took it back to its original Beaux-Arts décor, which included the simple but formal garden based on 1913 drawings original to the grounds.

The mansion is listed on the National Register of Historic Places.

There are lots of museums that exhibit a persona that encourages visitors to move about quietly and speak barely above a whisper.

The Great American Dollhouse Museum in Danville is not one of them.

With more than 200 antique and artisan dollhouses on display, visitors not only see incredible craftsmanship but get a wonderful history lesson. Not only are children impressed, but adults, too.

The historically correct stories that are told through the miniature villages and towns is such a subtle learning experience that everyone leaves with a better understanding of our countries evaluation.

Not lost here is the wow factor. The intricate detail created by the artists makes visitors wonder out loud, "How do they do it?"

Make no mistake about it, this is a place for boys as well as girls and adults. Just because it's about dollhouses, boys will equally enjoy this fun place.

56

Unlike many museums, particularly those who appeal to children, there is a play area in the 6,000 square foot building. Dollhouses and books offer them the opportunity of a hands-on experience. Some of the museum's exhibits even allow visitors to take a peek in from the backside.

The downtown Dollhouse Museum opened in October 2008, and the 1939 building that used to be a National Guard Armory, seems like a perfect fit. The high arched ceilings, composed of hardwood and iron girders, give visitors an airy, open feeling while browsing the aisles and aisles of unique miniatures.

Lori Kagan is the driving force of the museum and is continuously searching for new items to include.

The Dollhouse Museum also has a gift shop that includes new, vintage, antiques and artisan miniatures to go along with the traditional museum memorabilia for sale.

700 Capitol Avenue

Phone: 502/564-3449 for tour schedules

Open: 8:30 a.m.–3:30 p.m., Monday–Friday; 10 a.m.–2 p.m., Saturday; 1 p.m.–4 p.m., Sunday

Admission: FREE

Visitor's Information

CENTRAL

PLACE
ONE CENT
STAMP
HERE

Kentucky State Capitol
Frankfort, KY

PRINTED
IN
U.S.A.

101 MUST PLACES TO VISIT IN KENTUCKY

Visiting Kentucky's State Capitol may not be at the top of your list of places to visit and see, but it should be.

Located in Frankfort this combination of Greek architecture and French styling is a magnificent structure that more than holds its own with any other state in the country.

Built at a cost of $1.8 million from 1905 to 1909, its signature is the massive dome above a seven story high rotunda which features bigger-than-life sculptures of several well-known Kentuckians.

Abraham Lincoln stands directly in the center of the marble-floored rotunda, surrounded by Jefferson Davis, Alben Barkley, Dr. Ephraim McDowell, and Henry Clay.

A visit here causes you to pause and enjoy the surroundings and even to as-

cend the massive marble staircase that branches off in two directions. The stairs were modeled after the Paris Grand Opera House.

On the second floor are the Kentucky Supreme Court and the law library. Portraits of former Supreme Court justices are shown in the grand halls. It is said that when built the Supreme Court chambers was the most expensive room in the building, costing some $25,000. The feature element of this "show room" is the solid mahogany paneling and the beautiful coffered ceiling covered in metal leafing.

The nearby State Reception Room includes a hand-woven Austrian rug designed just for this room in 1910. Numerous paintings and murals all add to the ambiance of this fantastic building.

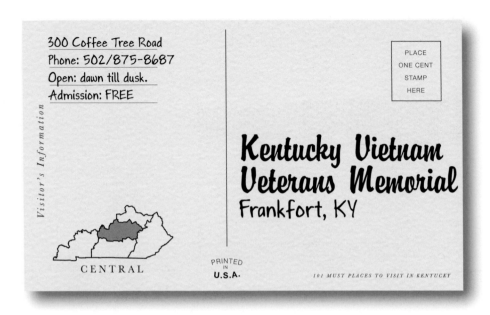

300 Coffee Tree Road
Phone: 502/875-8687
Open: dawn till dusk.
Admission: FREE

Visitor's Information

PLACE
ONE CENT
STAMP
HERE

Kentucky Vietnam Veterans Memorial
Frankfort, KY

CENTRAL

PRINTED
IN
U.S.A.

101 MUST PLACES TO VISIT IN KENTUCKY

Most everyone is aware of the Vietnam Memorial Wall in Washington, D.C., but there's a good chance that many Kentuckians have never visited Kentucky's tribute to those who made the ultimate sacrifice during the Vietnam War.

Recognized as one of the most original memorials in the nation, this beautiful memorial lists the names of the 1,103 Kentuckians lost in the war, including 23 missing in action.

The names are engraved into a granite plaza. The design concept is in the form of a large sundial. The stainless steel gnomon cast its shad-

ow onto the plaza and each name is placed so that the shadow's tip touches the name as it moves through the day's cycle.

The result is that on the anniversary of the veteran's death he or she has their own personal Memorial Day.

The location of each name is fixed mathematically by the date of the death, geographic location of the memorial, the height of the gnomon and the physics of solar movement. To further add to the work and thought that went into all of this, the stones were then designed and cut in a way that would not divide an individual's name.

The Kentucky Vietnam Veterans Memorial completed in 1988, is a quiet, respectful site as it should be. Many visitors come alone, or in small groups, or families.

Visitors can, if they look closely, follow a graphic history of the war and its intensity and duration. The dates and names are right there for you to see.

According to the state, this memorial, that first opened in November 1988, is now included on most visits to Frankfort by school children, providing a history lesson on the Vietnam War as well as an example of understanding how mathematics, science and physics have been combined to create this most worthy memorial that was created by Helm Roberts of Lexington.

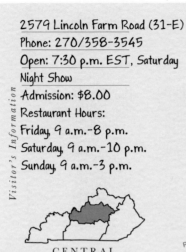

The entertainment at Joel Ray Sprowls Lincoln Jamboree in Hodgenville may not be up to the standards of the finals of American Idol, but then again to some it may be a whole lot better.

Dwight Eisenhower was president, a gallon of gas 25 cents, and a loaf of bread cost 25 cents, when Joel Ray opened his Lincoln Jamboree. It was September 11, 1954, and it's still going strong.

Joel Ray likes to say how "some said it wouldn't last." He also likes to tell corny jokes as he introduces the different singers of the future that appear on his stage. Those he has introduced in the past include Bill Anderson, Bill Grammer, Grandpa Jones, String Bean, Jerry Lee Lewis, The Oak Ridge Boys, Ernest Tubb, Cowboy Copas, Lorrie Morgan and Patty Ramey who later changed her name to Patty Loveless.

He'll also tell you there was one he missed on in 1960. Turned out he thought the

$100 fee for a young singer named Patsy Cline was too much.

When you walk into Joel Ray's lobby it's a combination restaurant and museum. The walls are jammed with his personal collections that include a larger than life statue of Elvis.

The Lincoln Jamboree is a family show that is fast-paced for about three hours, with a 20-minute intermission. No alcohol or vulgarity is permitted here.

Joel Ray serves as the shows MC and comedian, as well as personally auditioning every act.

The house band is five pieces plus two female singers, and their connections to Joel Ray is quite evident, as a couple have been playing there some 50 years.

Tours by appointment only
Phone: 859/744-4888 or
859/771-5406
Admission: donations accepted

Visitor's Information

CENTRAL

PLACE
ONE CENT
STAMP
HERE

Lower Howard's Creek
Winchester, KY

PRINTED
IN
U.S.A.

101 MUST PLACES TO VISIT IN KENTUCKY

This perhaps requires a little more effort to see than most of the listings in this book, but for those who are into raw bone history and walking hand-in-hand with Mother Nature, this is the place.

Lower Howard's Creek Nature and Heritage Preserve was officially established in 2001, but this beautiful landscape has been around much, much longer than that.

The approximately 300 acres is made up of a steep forested creek valley with limestone palisades, wildflowers, and a most unusual remnant of a late 18th and early 19th century industrial settlement. Visitors can see stone houses, mills, quarries and waterfalls. Five structures are listed on the National Register.

Lower Howard's Creek, named after John Howard back in 1775, is a study of early-day industry in the backwoods of Kentucky. The valley was abandoned by hu-

64

man occupation in the 1930s, and today is somewhat rugged, overgrown terrain. The forest growth seen today is not what the land's occupants experienced back before the turn of the century as the land had been cleared and was lived and worked on.

Old roads and rock fences that enclosed fields where livestock grazed, and, of course, Howard's Creek, that over centuries has cut its way through the limestone to create the steep-sided valley is evident.

This incredibly beautiful place needs to be seen with a tour guide in order to better interpret the valley's historical and environmental significance.

Public tours are held throughout the spring and early summer, and again in the fall and winter months. There is no bad time to visit Lower Howard's Creek although the middle of summer does create such a thick canopy that it is often difficult to see what is below.

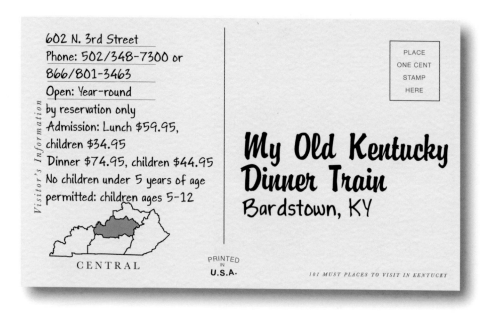

My Old Kentucky Dinner Train
Bardstown, KY

101 MUST PLACES TO VISIT IN KENTUCKY

Trains are nostalgic, especially when you consider that there are two generations now removed from the so-called heyday of passenger train travel. Today there is a certain mystic about the days when there were more people traveling by rail than on highways.

Since 1988 My Old Kentucky Diner Train has been providing visitors not only the opportunity to ride a train in fine style, but also to enjoy equally fine dining.

An excursion on the Dinner Train begins at an old renovated 1860 freight depot in Bardstown.

A pair of 1940 era diesel engines provides the power for the three spiffy dining cars once commonly used on passenger trains that traveled long distances.

The Dinner Train's two and a half hour route includes passing through the area's bourbon country, past Limestone Springs Junction, an old railroad depot. From there it's on to the edge of beautiful Bernheim Forest, near the former T.W. Samuels Distillery. The 35 mile roundtrip travels at a slow pace, so passengers can enjoy the scenery.

If you go in the evening, a five-course meal will be prepared in the train's traveling kitchen car.

The menu changes seasonally, but dinner choices include prime rib, poultry, pork, or seafood.

Lunch trips include a three-course meal.

My Old Kentucky Dinner Train is open year-round, but as might be expected the beautiful fall foliage is most visible during October.

The portion of the track the train travels on was originally called the Bardstown Branch Railroad, built in 1850. It connected to the Louisville and Nashville Railroad thus providing passenger and freight service to Bardstown. It was purchased by R.J. Corman Railroad who started the dinner train.

Throughout the year the Dinner Train offers passengers special events, such as "who done it" murder mysteries, Halloween, Thanksgiving, North Pole Express, Valentine, and Easter.

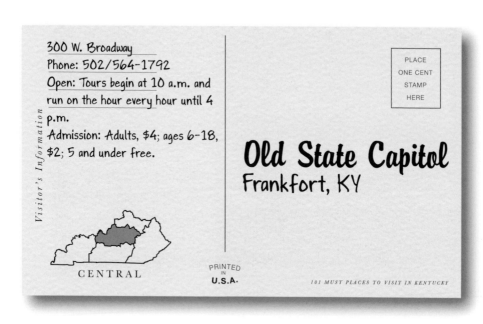

Visitor's Information

300 W. Broadway

Phone: 502/564-1792

Open: Tours begin at 10 a.m. and run on the hour every hour until 4 p.m.

Admission: Adults, $4; ages 6-18, $2; 5 and under free.

Old State Capitol
Frankfort, KY

CENTRAL

PRINTED
IN
U.S.A.

101 MUST PLACES TO VISIT IN KENTUCKY

As one might expect there are many things to see and do in Kentucky's capitol city of Frankfort. But one well worth the price of admission is the Old State Capitol, built in 1830 at a then-tidy sum of $85,000.

Listed as a National Historic Landmark, the Greek Revival structure, built of limestone walls and a copper roof is an architectural delight, particularly with the use of marble and its relationship in the incredible self-supporting curved, double staircase leading to the rotunda just below the domed cupola.

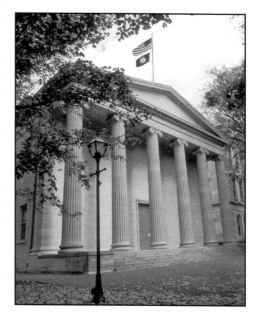

Several of the rooms have undergone restoration, but it's those original floors of Mercer County marble that give visitors a feel that this building will be here for years to come. It's a good thing because the first two buildings on this same spot were destroyed by fire.

Upstairs, two chambers, one for the Senate and one for the House of Representatives, are filled with replicas of desks and benches. Above each room hangs an original 500 pound chandelier.

In the ground floor area visitors can tour the old State Law Library. Reproductive furniture and period artifacts allow visitors a glimpse of what it was like for legislators to conduct state business in this venue from 1831-1910.

The Old State Capitol grounds are marked with a plaque identifying where William Goebel, from northern Kentucky, was assassinated walking to the Capitol on January 30, 1900, shortly after being elected Governor. History says it was the site of the only assassination of a United States governor.

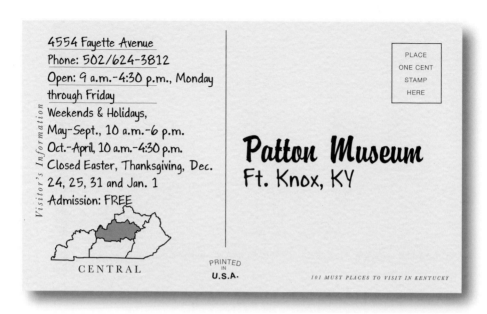

Commonly called the Patton Museum, this attraction has been around in one form or another since 1949.

George Patton was one of America's greatest and controversial generals. Born in 1885 in San Gabriel, California, he dreamed of making his mark on the battlefield. His enthusiasm for armor and how it could be developed to win battles set the standard for organization when it came to tank training.

As commander of the Third Army, his troops swept across France, Belgium, Luxembourg, Germany, Austria and Czechoslovakia, liber-

ating and conquering over 81,000 miles of land.

The Museum is dedicated to the preservation of the U.S. Army and its Armor Branch of military.

The Museum's campus houses display memorabilia of Gen. Patton's that is the largest collection of personal artifacts in the world.

Several galleries throughout the complex let visitors see how wars were fought. One pertains strictly to Patton while others showcase WWI, WWII, as well as past world wars.

World War I marked the beginning of mechanized armor warfare. The tank quickly became the most effective weapon on earth.

A wide array of weapons and armor are on display, as well as weapons and tanks used by our country's enemies.

Gen. Patton's legacy was further enhanced several years ago in the movie "Patton," and as a soldier's soldier, this museum allows visitors to learn much more about his accomplishments than can be seen on a Hollywood screen.

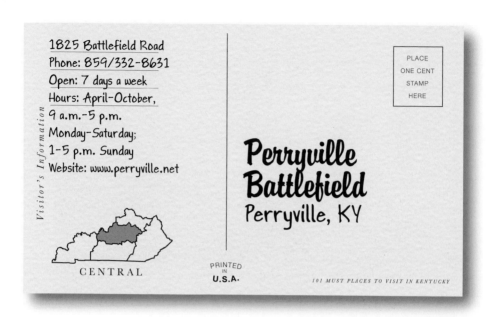

1825 Battlefield Road
Phone: 859/332-8631
Open: 7 days a week
Hours: April-October,
9 a.m.-5 p.m.
Monday-Saturday;
1-5 p.m. Sunday
Website: www.perryville.net

Visitor's Information

CENTRAL

PRINTED IN U.S.A.

Perryville Battlefield
Perryville, KY

PLACE ONE CENT STAMP HERE

101 MUST PLACES TO VISIT IN KENTUCKY

A visit to Perryville Battlefield today reveals very little of the horrific Civil War battle that took place on October 8, 1862.

Visitors can see one of the most pristine battlefields in the United States. Its mere presence, along with the town's historic merchant's row, makes this, not only a somber educational experience, but on the lighter side, a fun place to stroll around and shop.

The Battle of Perryville was the largest Civil War battle fought in

Kentucky, and historians have written that had the Confederate army and its 18,000 soldiers defeated the 20,000 Union troops, it could have altered the entire course of the Civil War.

The battle fought here was more than a battle for Kentucky; it was a battle for the nation.

Nearly 7,500 soldiers for both sides were either killed or wounded in the fight.

The park's museum displays and tells of the battle on that October day. It was the Confederates last major attempt to gain control of Kentucky.

The battlefield is one of the most unaltered of its kind in the nation. The same visitor and viewing sheds that you see today are what those 38,000 soldiers saw on that fateful day in 1862.

Self-guided walking tours are available. Every October the Civil War battle is reenacted, featuring authentic weaponry, clothing, campsites and military demonstrations.

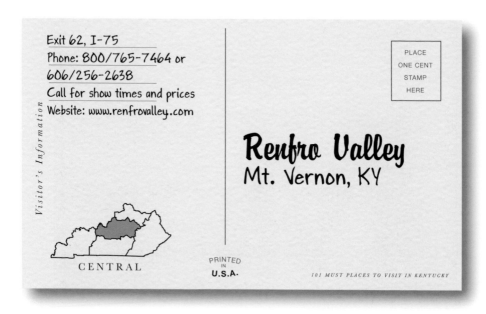

Exit 62, I-75
Phone: 800/765-7464 or
606/256-2638
Call for show times and prices
Website: www.renfrovalley.com

Visitor's Information

Renfro Valley
Mt. Vernon, KY

PLACE
ONE CENT
STAMP
HERE

CENTRAL

PRINTED
IN
U.S.A.

When John Lair built his 650-seat theater in a large wooden barn, at the edge of Mt. Vernon in Renfro Valley, he had a vision to help preserve Appalachian music and culture from what he perceived as the over-commercialization of country music.

The first radio broadcast was back in 1939, and today, Renfro Valley has not lost site of Mr. Lair's original mission.

Renfro Valley has been referred to as the place "where time stands still," and although such stars as George Jones, Aaron Tippin, Merle Haggard, Mickey Gilley, Ronnie Milsap, Connie Smith, Charley Pride, Lorrie Morgan, Carl Hurley and Loretta Lynn perform here, there is no doubt that the real star is the show itself.

Renfro Valley presents a variety of entertainment, alternating shows that feature bluegrass, folk, gospel, old-time country, mountain clogging, and, of course, down-home hillbilly humor.

The show schedule runs from March through December.

Renfro Valley is also home to the Kentucky Music Hall of Fame and Museum. It is a 17,000-square-foot facility that pays homage to Kentucky's music history, dating back to the 1700s to the present. It's range of inductees run from Bill Monroe, the "father of bluegrass music," to jazz musician Lionel Hampton.

The variety of music and entertainers here is unparallel in Kentucky, and it's easy to understand what John Lair was talking about years ago when he said his radio program was the only one where you can hear "Rock of Ages," and "Turkey in the Straw," on the same program, and neither is out of place.

109 Buffalo Creek Drive (Just off
I-65 at Exit 94
Phone: 270/234-1100
Open: Year-round: Monday-
Saturday, 10 a.m.-6 p.m.
Sunday, 1 p.m.-5 p.m.
Closed all major holidays
Admission: $5 adults; $4 seniors;
Pre-Schoolers Free
Website: www.schmidtmuseum.com

Visitor's Information

PLACE
ONE CENT
STAMP
HERE

Schmidt Museum
of Coca-Cola
Memorabilia
Elizabethtown, KY

CENTRAL

PRINTED
IN
U.S.A.

101 MUST PLACES TO VISIT IN KENTUCKY

A s soon as visitors drive into the parking lot at the Coca-Cola Museum in Elizabethtown, they can't help but notice the large hand protruding from the side of the metal building. In the hand is, what else, but a bottle of Coke.

What you see on the outside is only a small sampling of what's inside.

This is the largest privately owned collection of Coca-Cola memorabilia in the world, and this 32,000 square-foot facility, which opened at its present location in 2005, pays homage to the world's most recognizable trademark.

Here, it's much more than bottles and cans. It's trucks, vans, clocks, calendars, clothes, vending machines, glass wear, trays, and even an 1893 soda fountain. There's well over 80,000 items in this rare collection.

Bill Schmidt, a third generation Coca-Cola bottler, and his wife Jan, began putting their collection together in 1971. In the beginning it was just to decorate their then new bottling plant. But, before you can say, "another Coke, please," the collection had taken on a life of its own.

Not long after they had made space available in the plant, and after some 25 years, more than a million visitors from throughout the world had seen their collection. By then they were filling warehouses.

Due to safety regulations, the museum closed for awhile. But now visitors can stroll through this climate controlled venue and not only see but learn the history of this icon of a beverage.

A bit of trivia: Until 1908, the military restricted the consumption of Coca-Cola, and then years later Gen. Dwight D. Eisenhower ordered 10 complete Coca-Cola Bottling Plants shipped to North Africa as soon as his troops landed. Later 54 more were shipped to various locations wherever the troops went.

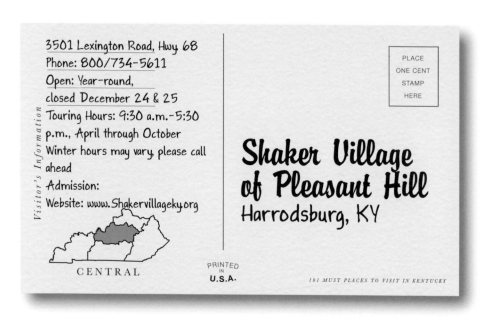

3501 Lexington Road, Hwy 68
Phone: 800/734-5611
Open: Year-round,
closed December 24 & 25
Touring Hours: 9:30 a.m.–5:30
p.m., April through October
Winter hours may vary, please call
ahead
Admission:
Website: www.Shakervillageky.org

Visitor's Information

Shaker Village of Pleasant Hill
Harrodsburg, KY

CENTRAL

PRINTED IN U.S.A.

PLACE ONE CENT STAMP HERE

101 MUST PLACES TO VISIT IN KENTUCKY

Just getting to Shaker Village makes this visit worthwhile. Whether coming from Lexington or Harrodsburg, the drive on Highway 68 is beautiful. Vistas of rolling hills, dry-stacked rock fences, old farm houses and twisting turns force you to slow down and enjoy the ride.

Shaker Village of Pleasant Hill is the epitome of preservation. The Shakers arrived here in 1805, and settled on some 4,000 acres rising just above the Kentucky River. In its day Pleasant Hill was a thriving agricultural community with as many as 500 residents.

By 1910, however, only a few Shakers had survived and the village shut down.

In 1961 a preservation group set about to reclaim Pleasant Hill, and what visitors see today is astounding. Thirty-three of the original buildings and structures have been restored, and 2,700 acres of farmland preserved.

The "official" name of the sect was The United Society of Believers in Christ's Second Appearing. However, because of their spiritual dance, they became known as Shakers. Their communal society promoted a peaceful existence, and earned a well-deserved reputation for being innovative when it came to labor-saving inventions.

Brooms and fine furniture is just a couple of items the Shakers are known for.

Today's Shaker Village allows visitors to tour at their own pace, viewing the actual crafting of broom makers, coopers, spinners and weavers. Although soaking up a lot of history, one of the highlights here is sitting down at the Trustee's Office Inn for a hearty breakfast, lunch or dinner. Some, of which, are prepared with original Shaker recipes.

Also note that there are 80 guest rooms, furnished in Shaker reproductions, available for overnights. Each is air-conditioned, with private bath and television.

Phone: 606/305-8636 or
606/875-6605

PLACE
ONE CENT
STAMP
HERE

Visitor's Information

Somernite Cruise
Somerset, KY

CENTRAL

PRINTED
IN
U.S.A.

101 MUST PLACES TO VISIT IN KENTUCKY

Since 2000 Somernite has been putting on a car show, not just any car show mind you, but one that attracts show cars and spectators from several states away.

Back then several local "car guys" got together and decided they wanted to put together a car show so they wouldn't have to drive all the way to Pigeon Forge, Tennessee.

The rest is history.

Now the show, appropriately called Somernite Cruise, is held each

summer over a seven month period. Running from April through October, every fourth Saturday of the month, the event attracts as many as 1,500 classic cars each time. In all, cars from 27 states have participated in the cruise-in, with some coming from as far away as Florida, Alabama, Texas, North Dakota, and even Hawaii and Canada.

Each of the monthly car shows actually begin on Thursday night at a local Dairy Queen. Friday nights see things pick up a bit with a rock and roll block party at the local Wal-Mart.

But Saturday is the day. All kinds of cruises, "show & shines," food vendors and music line the Somerset downtown area.

It might be a good idea when you go to this event to make sure you throw in a couple of lawn chairs in case you want to join the thousands of locals who line the boulevard to sit and watch all of those beautiful memories cruise by.

Lots of towns in Kentucky have nice little car shows, but Somernite Cruise has taken it to the next level as recognition in the form of car magazines and television shows have put Somerset on the map nationally.

Phone: 800/755-0076
Website: www.gabbf.org

Visitor's Information

The Great American Brass Band Festival
Danville, KY

CENTRAL

PRINTED
IN
U.S.A.

101 MUST PLACES TO VISIT IN KENTUCKY

For four days every June, the town of Danville is alive with the sound of music. The beautiful campus of Centre College since 1990 has been the primary location for the main portion of The Great American Brass Band Festival.

The emphasis is on brass, and some of the best national performers and international musicians are on hand for this unique festival.

Although this charming event is all about music, there are a multitude of other things to entertain families: Chautaqua Teas; a Beer,

Bourbon and Brass event at the Beaumont Inn in nearby Harrodsburg; a Brass History Conference; a concert at Old Fort Harrod, also in Harrodsburg; a Brass Master class; Main Street Parade; Great American Balloon Race; and, what many consider the highlight of the festival, The Great American Picnic.

At the picnic, hundreds and hundreds of people set up tables with their own food of choice, while thousands fill the rolling lawns of the campus with chairs and blankets as they watch and listen to the more-than 60 bands and performers throughout the day and into the evening.

The ambience of the college, which dates back to 1819, Danville's beautiful downtown, and elegant homes make this a really enjoyable event to be a part of.

Food vendors, artists, garden shops, and galleries featuring various crafts are offered for those who want to take a break and stroll the downtown area.

1001 Cherry Blossom Way
Phone: 502/868-3027 or
800/866-4485
Open: Mon-Fri, 9 a.m.—4 p.m.
with extended hours to 7 p.m. on
Thur. Plant Tours: 10 a.m., noon,
2 p.m., Mon-Fri with 6 p.m. on
Thur.
Closed holidays
Admission: FREE

CENTRAL

PLACE
ONE CENT
STAMP
HERE

Toyota Plant Tour
Georgetown, KY

PRINTED
IN
U.S.A.

101 MUST PLACES TO VISIT IN KENTUCKY

O utside of Japan, Toyota Motor Manufacturing in Georgetown is the company's largest manufacturing plant in the world.

And what a plant it is.

Over 7,000 people are employed at this seven and a half million square foot facility. To put the size in perspective, the floor space is equivalent to 156 football fields.

When visitors come here they don't have to worry about walking in this massive layout, because all of the tours are conducted in comfortable trams.

The plant tour experience begins in the 11,500 square foot visitor's center that first opened in 1994. There, the very first Camry to roll off the assembly line can be seen, as well as interactive exhibits, which even include several Toyotas for visitors to get in and out of, slam doors, flip knobs and recline the seats. You'll also hear the history of Toyota and see a video of the company's first car arriving in America.

Each tram has a tour guide that explains what you are seeing in this ultra-modern facility that turns out two new Toyotas every 55 seconds.

Even though the tours began in 1994, actual production began in 1988 with the Toyota Camry sedan. The Avalon sedan came on in 1994, and the Sienna minivan was produced from 1997 to 2002.

Toyota's automotive plant tour is considered one of the best in the world, and on top of it all it's free.

Visitors should allow one and a half to two hours for the entire experience.

No photo taking devices, including cell phones are permitted on the tour. Neither are purses, hand bags, back packs, or briefcases. A valid photo is required and children with families must be first grade age or above.

Reservations are required, but walk-up will be accommodated if space is available.

O riginally named Clermont, and consisting of seven rooms, this now 44-room mansion is one of the most incredible homes in Kentucky.

Considered a fine example of Italianate architecture, this over-10,000 square foot home is made even more significant because of the early-day technology used when it was added on to in 1861-1862.

At that time it was renamed White Hall.

General Green Clay had owned Clermont, was a friend of Daniel Boone's, and had amassed quite a fortune for that day and time in Kentucky. His possessions included several distilleries, taverns, farms, and even a ferry on the Kentucky River.

It was Gen. Clay's son, Cassius, who took Clermont and turned it into White Hall.

Along with the transition of the home came a central heating system that was supplied by a pair of basement fireboxes. The heat rose up and into the rooms through ducts to open-

ings cut out in the numerous fire places.

Another "comfort of home" feature was the home's indoor plumbing. Rainwater would be collected in a large cistern on the third floor and then fed into the water closet, bath, and commode on the floor below.

Following the death of Cassius M. Clay, White Hall's ownership stayed in the family until the state purchased it in 1967. Soon after, Kentucky Governor Louie B. Nunn and his wife Beulah led the effort to restore the beautiful home.

In 1971 White Hall was opened for tours.

The home sits on 13 acres and displays several other historical buildings that include a stone building, formerly used as a kitchen and loom house. Also, there is an ice house, chicken house, smoke house, and blacksmith shop.

Today, some even say White Hall is haunted. It is a common occurrence for "ghost hunters" to ask permission to do research.

www.kentuckywine.com

PLACE
ONE CENT
STAMP
HERE

Winery Tours
Kentucky

CENTRAL

PRINTED
IN
U.S.A.

101 MUST PLACES TO VISIT IN KENTUCKY

O f course everyone knows about bourbon and its connection to Kentucky. But what many are finding out is that wine – yes wine, has been around for almost as long.

The first vineyard in Kentucky was planted in 1798, and over the next century the state was among the top three wine producers in the country.

However, it all came to an end with prohibition in the 1920s.

Throughout the state, wineries are making a comeback.

Some of today's vineyards are former tobacco farms whose owners are trying new crops, and because of the growing interest in wine and vineyards, the state even has a grape and wine marketing specialist.

Many of Kentucky's wineries sell their product, offer tours, and provide food and entertainment. Fun places to visit.

All wines start at the vineyard, where the process actually begins with a delicate balance between the sun and the soil.

After that it goes something like this:

Packed grapes are delivered to a winery where they are gently squeezed. Juices then go to a holding tank where it is chilled, thus allowing for sediment from the grapes to drop to the bottom of the tank. The clean juice is then combined with yeast, and for the next few weeks fermentation takes place at somewhere near 60 degrees. Some wines are fermented in oak barrels for added flavor. Once fermentation is complete, the wine is chilled for clarification and then filtered into bottles.

There are some 30 wineries in Central Kentucky. There are also wine tours in Eastern, South Central and Western Kentucky.

It is suggested that you call ahead to make sure they are open during your planned travels.

For a directory of wineries go to www.kentuckywine.com.

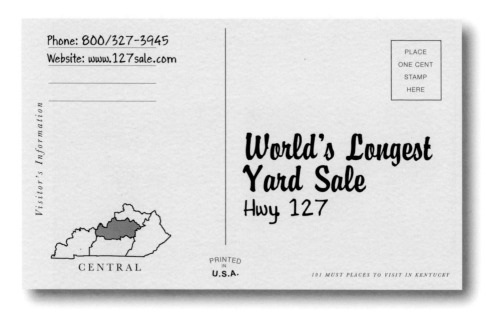

Every early August over 3,000 vendors line up along Highway 127 from Defiance, Ohio in the north all the way to Gadsden, Alabama in the south, to sell almost everything imaginable in what is billed as the "World's Longest Yard Sale."

For some 630 miles of back roads that wind and twist through Ohio, Kentucky, Tennessee, Georgia and Alabama, thousands of cars, trucks, vans, and almost anything with a motor, huffs and puffs to a slow crawl as shoppers look for a spot to pull over.

Route 127 is posted with Longest Yard Sale signs that help travelers traverse the almost continuous line of pop-up tents, tables full of cookie jars, lamps, golf clubs and old picture frames. Everyone is looking for that "can't live without find." The World's Longest Yard Sale is full of items shoppers didn't know they needed until they saw it.

This event was originally organized in order to get travelers off the interstates and onto the rural back roads. As word spread, more people began to set up tables with "stuff" to sell. And with more people selling, more people buying were showing up.

Private homes, church and shopping center parking lots, almost anywhere that offers a decent place to pull several cars over, becomes a part of this phenomenon. People come from as far away as California just to be a part of the hunt. There are so many at certain times of the day that traffic almost comes to a standstill.

In Kentucky, Highway 127 runs from Covington in northern Kentucky and exits the state at Albany in the south.

A good state map comes in handy, even if you just stay in Kentucky. Perhaps even planning for an overnight in advance will make this event more restful. Patience is urged and extreme caution should be the norm when pulling off the road and re-entering.

Towns along the way include Owenton, Frankfort, Lawrenceburg, Harrodsburg, Danville, Liberty, Russell Springs and Jamestown.

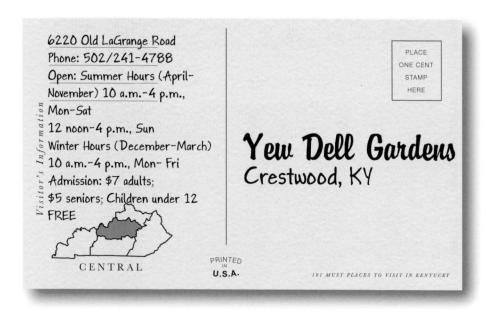

6220 Old LaGrange Road
Phone: 502/241-4788
Open: Summer Hours (April–
November) 10 a.m.–4 p.m.,
Mon–Sat
12 noon–4 p.m., Sun
Winter Hours (December–March)
10 a.m.–4 p.m., Mon– Fri
Admission: $7 adults;
$5 seniors; Children under 12
FREE

Visitor's Information

CENTRAL

PLACE
ONE CENT
STAMP
HERE

Yew Dell Gardens

Crestwood, KY

PRINTED
IN
U.S.A.

101 MUST PLACES TO VISIT IN KENTUCKY

S ome might refer to Yew Dell Gardens as a bit of heaven. For sure this 33-acre botanical garden is a special place.

The Garden's beginning dates back to 1941 when Theodore and Martha Lee Klein bought the Oldham County property, and set out to turn it into a premier collection of some of the most unusual plants found anywhere in the United States.

For over 60 years the Klein's passion for the place was well documented. Their collection of over a thousand unusual specimen trees and shrubs, as well as the development of new plant varieties has laid

the foundation for what can be seen in Yew Dell Gardens today.

Theodore Klein's gardens cover a wide range of styles. Yew Dell's signature is the Serpentine Garden, but also quite popular is the formal topiary garden, and the English Walled Garden.

Klein died in 1998, but what he did here was so spectacular that local and national garden organizations stepped forward to ensure that his efforts would live on.

And they have.

Today, continual experimentation with new and better plant varieties is one of the norms. The Yew Dell staff has a working relationship with several commercial nurseries, and the venue sponsors several educational programs on plants, gardens and gardening for professionals as well as those who just enjoy gardening.

Not to be overlooked here are the eye-pleasing stone buildings that create a campus-like effect in the garden. There is also an abundance of benches that seemed to be placed in just the right spots to make you want to slow down a bit.

Open to the public are events that include the annual Twilight in the Garden Gala, Plant Sale & Garden Market, workshops, and weekly guided tours.

American Printing House for the Blind	Louisville, Ky
Belle of Louisville	Louisville, Ky
Brown Hotel	Louisville, Ky
Cave Hill Cemetery	Louisville, Ky
Churchill Downs	Louisville, Ky
Falls of the Ohio	Clarksville, In
Frazier International History Museum	Louisville, Ky
Great Train Expo	Louisville, Ky
Jefferson Memorial Forest	Fairdale, Ky
Joe Ley Antiques	Louisville, Ky
Kentucky Show	Louisville, Ky
Kentucky State Fair	Louisville, Ky
Louisville Slugger Museum	Louisville, Ky
Louisville Zoo	Louisville, Ky
Muhammad Ali Center	Louisville, Ky
National Farm Machinery Show	Louisville, Ky
Saint James Court Art Fair	Louisville, Ky

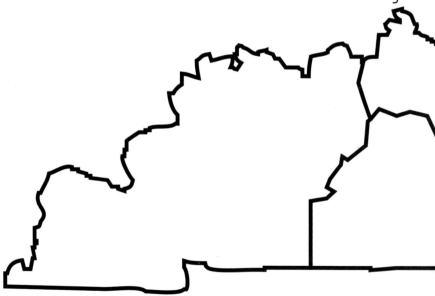

Louisville Region

Saint X–Trinity Football Game	Louisville, Ky
Seelbach Hotel	Louisville, Ky
Speed Art Museum	Louisville, Ky
Thunder Over Louisville	Louisville, Ky
Waverly Hills Sanatorium	Louisville, Ky
Zachary Taylor Cemetery	Louisville, Ky

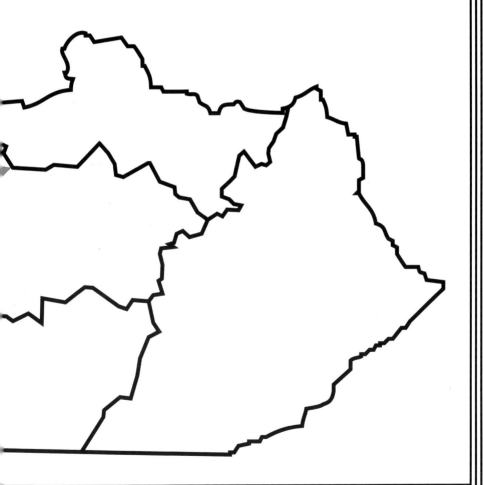

Visitor's Information

1839 Frankfort Avenue
Phone: 800/223-1839 or
502/895-2405
Open: 8:30 a.m.-4:30 p.m.,
Monday through Friday
10 a.m.-3 p.m., Saturday
Tours: 10 a.m. and 2 p.m.,
Monday through Thursday
Admission: FREE

LOUISVILLE

PLACE
ONE CENT
STAMP
HERE

American Printing House for the Blind
Louisville, KY

PRINTED
IN
U.S.A.

101 MUST PLACES TO VISIT IN KENTUCKY

The world's largest creator of educational material for the blind, this one-of-a-kind facility takes up nearly a city block of space.

Opened in 1883, adjacent to the Kentucky School for the Blind, today it provides specialized materials, products, and product-related services needed for education and life. Some 300 people are employed here in the production of publications in Braille, large type, recorded, and computer disc formats, tactile globes, maps, board games, specialized tests, and talking software.

In 1994, the American Printing House opened an award-winning museum that offers visitors an opportunity to explore the efforts of generations of blind individuals, teachers, and inventors to overcome obstacles to learning. A book being printed on a century-old Braille press can be seen, and then the latest computer technology is shown in today's printing.

96

Visitors can write their name in Braille, and tour a working studio where "talking books" are produced. There are eleven recording studios here.

The 250,000 square-foot facility is unique to the nation in its mission to serve over a million people in the United States who are blind, and another four million who are visually impaired.

The fact that the American Printing House for the Blind is open for public tours is also unique in itself.

The American Printing House is located in the historic Frankfort Avenue district of Louisville, and is convenient to places to eat and other things to see.

Phone: 866/832-0011
401 W. River Road, Downtown

PLACE
ONE CENT
STAMP
HERE

Visitor's Information

Belle of Louisville
Louisville, KY

LOUISVILLE

PRINTED
IN
U.S.A.

101 MUST PLACES TO VISIT IN KENTUCKY

According to Mayor Jerry Abramson, The *Belle of Louisville* is the oldest authentic Mississippi River-style steamboat operating in the world today.

Although the paddlewheel steamboat was built in 1914, it hasn't always been called the *Belle*. Initially named the *Idlewild*, and then the *Avalon*, it didn't become the *Belle of Louisville* until 1962, when it was purchased at a bankruptcy auction in Cincinnati for $34,000.

The City of Louisville was in search for a landmark, something that could be easily seen and perhaps even draw tourist. The old boat seemed like a natural, and Jefferson County Judge Executive Marlow Cook sort of went out on a limb with the purchase.

Judge Cook was prepared to bid up to $40,000 for what was hoped would become a stationary river museum. For the boat to actually cruise again would be the ultimate.

Much of Louisville's history is tied to the Ohio River, and for over a decade the city had been without a boat of substantial size, and there was a definite interest in revitalizing a neglected riverfront.

For Judge Cook, who later became a U.S. Senator, changing the name from *Avalon* to The *Belle of Louisville* was a mere simple process. His wife Nancy had attended an Eastern girl's college, where her southern ways and charm earned her the nickname, Belle. The *Avalon* soon officially became the *Belle of Louisville.*

The *Belle* is a focal point for Louisville thanks to Marlow Cook and his supporters. There were some, however, who weren't overly excited about the purchase, so whenever a disgruntled citizen stopped by his office to complain, the judge would reach in a jar on his desk and pull out six pennies to give to the person. That, according to Cook, was how much it cost each Jefferson County citizen.

Today the *Belle* represents the good times, steamboat races, festivals, cruises, dances, weddings, receptions and parties. The familiar sound of its whistle and melodic tunes from the calliope convey to visitors another era . . . an era that still belongs to Louisville.

Capacity is just under 1,000. Call for tour times and prices.

335 W. Broadway
Phone: 502/583-1234 or
888/888-5252

Visitor's Information

Brown Hotel
Louisville, KY

LOUISVILLE

PRINTED
IN
U.S.A.

101 MUST PLACES TO VISIT IN KENTUCKY

O pened in 1923 at a cost of $4 million, this 16-story hotel has gained a reputation as one of the finest lodging establishments in the south.

Louisville businessman James Graham Brown built the downtown hotel, and like many intercity hotels, experienced its share of ups and downs. Prohibition, the Great Depression and the 1937 flood each took their shots at the Brown, and even after closing its doors in 1971, was able to make a return.

For several years the property served as the headquarters for Louisville Public Schools. But all would not be lost on this stately property, and a few years later it was completely renovated and reopened as the grand

100

hotel in which it was intended. The architecture is incredible.

Located at the corner of Fourth and Broadway, the hotel was and is a social hotbed, particularly during Derby Week. Its guest list over the years included President Harry Truman, Elizabeth Taylor, Joan Crawford, Eddie Cantor, Gene Autry, Eva Marie Saint, Robert Young, George Gobel, Queen Elizabeth, Gene Krupa, Dan Rowen and Dick Martin.

A few years ago the hotel was featured in the film "Elizabethtown" that starred Orlando Bloom and Kirsten Dunst, and before he became a famous actor, Louisville native Victor Mature was an elevator operator at the hotel.

Even though the Brown Hotel is known for high-style, and southern traditional hospitality, it is also known as the place where the Hot Brown was first introduced.

In 1926 hotel chef Fred Schmidt first put the open-faced sandwich together, consisting of turkey and bacon, topped with cheese and tomato. Today it is a staple of many southern restaurants, particularly those in Kentucky.

The lobby of the Brown Hotel has been described by several publications as having a lavish lobby that looks as though it came straight from a 1930s movie set.

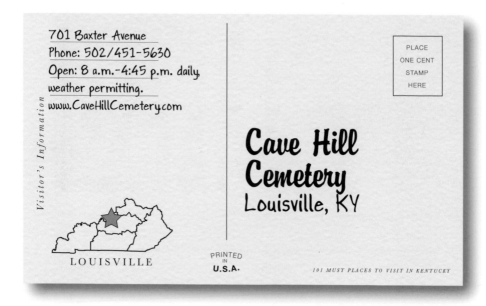

701 Baxter Avenue

Phone: 502/451-5630

Open: 8 a.m.-4:45 p.m. daily,

weather permitting.

www.CaveHillCemetery.com

Visitor's Information

Cave Hill Cemetery
Louisville, KY

LOUISVILLE

PRINTED
IN
U.S.A.

101 MUST PLACES TO VISIT IN KENTUCKY

A cemetery in a "Must Places to Visit Before You Die" book with "before" being the operative word might seem out of place, but not Cave Hill Cemetery in Louisville.

Cave Hill is a 300-acre horticultural paradise to many who visit, often times several times a year. But try telling birdwatchers it's all about flowers and trees, and you'll get the "do not go there" without your binoculars pitch.

If you are a first time visitor a slow drive through the grounds and its 16 miles of paved roadways is suggested in order for you to get a feel for the vastness of the cemetery. At the same time it will provide you with certain areas that really, really interest you.

Some say the spring time is the best time to visit Cave Hill. Early risers, like daffodils, crocuses, and, of course, dogwoods are among the flowers and trees that jump start this beautiful cemetery.

This is an outdoor museum, with thousands of exquisite monumental works of art. Opened in 1848, then on the outskirts of Louisville, today it is an island of peace, surrounded by the city's hustle and bustle.

Cave Hill is considered one of the finest arboretums in the nation, and its 500 varieties of trees and shrubs blend in with the five lakes and a quarry to make this a "must visit."

If you decide to park your car and stroll the grounds, you are sure to discover the real reason for Cave Hill's existence. The names and dates on the incredible, decorative monuments of all shapes and sizes reveal the history of old Louisville.

This cemetery is so popular among the locals that Cave Hill actually promotes spring tours: walking, geological, and twilight driving. The dates might change from year-to-year so you'll want to check out their website. The tours generally last two hours and range in fees of $25-$35. The driving tour is actually on a tractor-driven hay wagon.

Among the notables buried here, and there are many, are Col. Harland Sanders and George Rogers Clark.

Fall tours are also available, and reservations can be made by calling 502/451-5630.

Visitors are asked to remember that this is a cemetery and certain regulations and rules must be followed: no picnicking, no pets, no bicycles or motorcycles, no jogging, no buses or motor homes, and please do not park on the grass.

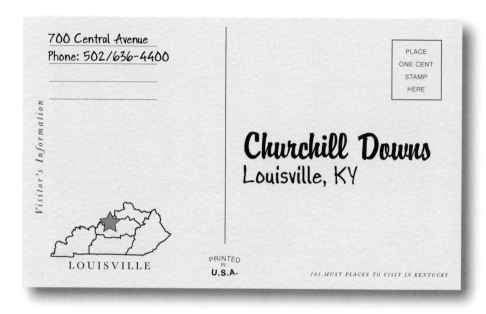

700 Central Avenue
Phone: 502/636-4400

Visitor's Information

Churchill Downs
Louisville, KY

LOUISVILLE

PRINTED
IN
U.S.A.

101 MUST PLACES TO VISIT IN KENTUCKY

There are many ways to experience Churchill Downs, one of which is the Kentucky Derby. This landmark thoroughbred race track, in south Louisville, is considered the premier such venue in America.

Of course, it is indeed the Kentucky Derby that has given the track its notoriety. First run in 1875, the Derby is considered one of the most recognizable sporting events in the world. Few probably realize that before 1900 there were four racetracks operating in Louisville. After all, this was a period in history that the horse was one of the most important elements in the country. In the beginning the Derby was run at a distance of $1\frac{1}{2}$ miles. A few years later the race was scaled back to its current $1\frac{1}{4}$ mile.

At one time the State Fair was even here.

The twin spires that sit atop of the grandstand section, and although not as prominent as they once were, are still the most recognizable architectural features of Churchill Downs.

The entire Churchill Downs complex that once was on 80 acres now covers some 147 acres. And although it is common for crowds to surpass 150,000 on Derby Day, the actual seating capacity is only 51,000. The added numbers come from tickets being sold as standing room only to the paddock area and infield. Please be advised that on Derby Day the infield is not for the faint-of-heart.

Although the Kentucky Derby is always run the first Saturday of each May, another race, the Kentucky Oaks, is run the day before, on Friday. It, too, has become a 100,000 plus fan day.

The track also plays host to major concerts.

The Kentucky Derby Museum, opened in 1985, sits directly in front of Churchill Downs and is open year-round, where as Churchill is actually open for spring and fall racing only.

The Museum tells the storied history of both the Derby and Churchill Downs. Several exhibits that showcase training and racing of thoroughbred horses are included. But one of the features is a 360-degree cinema that shows a fast-paced documentary of the Kentucky Derby. It puts you right on the rail.

Falls of the Ohio
Clarksville, IN

101 MUST PLACES TO VISIT IN KENTUCKY

T his is an exception to all of the "must places to visit" in this book. Although listed as an Indiana attraction, to Kentuckians, and particularly those in Louisville, it is of utmost importance.

Without the Falls of the Ohio in this one spot, there's a good chance the city of Louisville might not be in existence. In the late 18th century and early to late 19th century, river traffic on the Ohio had to slow down

and often stop in order to rely on the "locals" to assist in navigating the 26-foot drop that included a series of rapids on the river.

Falls of the Ohio, in Clarksville, Indiana is a part of the Indiana State Park system and what it offers is something Hoosiers have known for a long time, and that this is a great place to visit.

Many Kentuckians are unaware that this is a relatively safe place to paddle in a canoe or kayak, and have a skyline view of Louisville's downtown. There is no barge traffic in this area of the river.

Other than being an unusual place to visit, this attraction of nature's creation shows off fossil beds not often seen.

The fossil beds are proof that an ocean existed here more than 350 million years ago in what is now Clark County, Indiana and Jefferson County, Kentucky.

Today visitors can enjoy and photograph what is said to be the largest exposed fossil reef in the world. Over 220 acres are exposed.

The Falls of the Ohio are also quite a nature habitat. Birds like blue herons and double-crested cormorants are commonly seen picking and pecking their way across the fossil beds in search of eats.

Call the park for information on guided tours both in and out of the water.

829 W. Main Street
(corner 9th & Main, Downtown)
Phone: 502/753-5663 or
866/886-7103
Open: Monday-Saturday,
9 a.m.-5 p.m.,
Sunday, noon-5 p.m.
Admission: $9

Visitor's Information

LOUISVILLE

Frazier International History Museum
Louisville, KY

PRINTED IN U.S.A.

101 MUST PLACES TO VISIT IN KENTUCKY

The Frazier International History Museum offers a glimpse of history that dates as far back as 1,000 years and involves a collaboration of museums on two continents.

A partnership between the Frazier Museum and the Royal Armories, Britain's oldest museum, allows for the Louisville venue to provide displays of the arms and armor of knights and kings, as well as the possessions of Henry VIII and Elizabeth I. Through its partnership with the British Royal Armories, the Frazier is the only museum outside Great Britain to host these exhibits and artifacts.

The Museum is known for its world-class collection of very rare pieces from throughout Europe, some dating back 1,000 years.

Visitors here will not only see the Royal Armories collection, which also includes the Tower of

London, but magnificent exhibits of American artifacts from the colonial period to the early 1900s. Many pieces on display were once in the possession of famous explorers, soldiers, politicians and celebrities.

Along with this priceless collection, the museum has multi-media and interactive displays. This state-of-the-art museum lets visitors experience, through the performances by costumed interpreters, live demonstrations of the use of arms and armor.

Owsley Brown Frazier began collecting historical arms over 30 years ago after inheriting a Kentucky Long Rifle from his grandfather, and today his priceless collections that have turned into a major tourist draw, is considered one of the anchor attractions in downtown Louisville.

Also included in the collection is a flintlock rifle belonging to George Washington, and Teddy Roosevelt's African safari hunting rifle.

Self-guided tours are the norm, but guided tours can be arranged. A gift shop and café is available.

Kentucky International Convention
Center
221 S. Fourth Street
Phone: 630/608-4988 or
502/595-4381
Mid-January
Open: 10 a.m.-4 p.m., Saturday
and Sunday
Admission: Adults $7, kids under
12 FREE

LOUISVILLE

PRINTED
IN
U.S.A.

PLACE
ONE CENT
STAMP
HERE

Great Train Expo
Louisville, KY

101 MUST PLACES TO VISIT IN KENTUCKY

A national traveling model train show makes this book because it is both unusual and unique for things to see and do.

The Great Train Expo comes to Louisville once a year for two days, usually in mid-January. The Kentucky International Convention Center has been the site as of late.

Usually for a father and son there is nothing better than looking at,

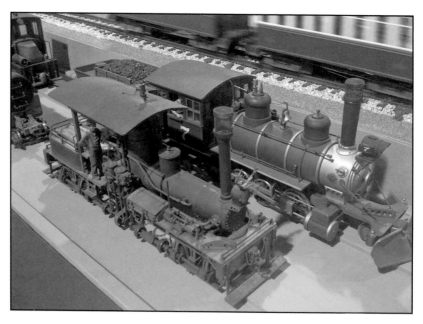

 or even playing with, a model train together. At the Great Train Expo this happens in a big way.

Every size and gauge trains are on display from HO, to Lionel, to American Flyer, to others. This event offers displays, vendors and even hands-on exhibits. What a place to gather ideas for track layouts to be used in your home.

Another unique thing about this show is that you can also sell your trains and even get them appraised.

Anything dealing with model trains can be purchased here to include hobby tools, die-cast vehicles, train whistlers, scenery items, videos, and more.

This event has been coming to Louisville for over 25 years and attracts several thousand visitors.

The Great Train Expo is ultra kid-friendly. There is a toy train play area, a model railroad layout that can be operated, workshops, and plenty of easy-to-see displays.

Jefferson Memorial Forest
Fairdale, KY

LOUISVILLE

PRINTED
IN
U.S.A.

101 MUST PLACES TO VISIT IN KENTUCKY

Just 20 minutes from downtown Louisville is a real treasure, Jefferson Memorial Forest. With more than 35 miles of hiking trails, ranging from the Siltstone Trail (a rugged 6.2 miles one way), to the Tulip Tree Trail (paved 0.2 miles one way), this 6,200 acre forest is considered the largest municipal urban forest in the United States.

The forest was established as a tribute to Kentucky's Armed Service veterans, and has been designated as a National Audubon Society Wildlife Refuge.

One of the focal points of the preserve is Tom Wallace Lake. Over 7-acres in size, it is stocked annually with trout and catfish. The lake features a handicapped-accessible fishing dock and nature trail. Both camping and fishing are permitted.

A nice feature at Jefferson Memorial Forest is the welcome center, an old county schoolhouse, built in 1916.

Some fifty types of trees,

including 10 species of oaks, have been identified. The forest is flush with a rich flora of wildflowers, and 17 species of ferns.

Several of the trails offer hikers a view of downtown Louisville.

Depending on the time of day, visitors can often spot a wide variety of animals in the wild. Bobcats, coyotes, gray and red foxes, white-tailed deer, minks, great blue herons and horned owls are the most prevalent.

It is essential that hikers remain on the respective trails and take no shortcuts. Picking of plants is not permitted, but visitors are encouraged to take pictures of this beautiful forest.

Today the renovated welcome center offers up a gift shop, rest-rooms, a comfortable stone fireplace and reservation office. Upstairs is a 30-seat meeting room.

For sure Jefferson Memorial Forest is probably not prominent on many Kentuckians minds, at least outside of Jefferson County. But now some of that may change.

Directions: From I-65 take I-265 West (Gene Snyder Freeway); take the New Cut Road exit and turn left; approximately 1.2 miles to yellow light, turn right onto Mitchell Hill road; 1.5 miles to welcome center.

T his museum-like retail store is a little bit of everything and any-thing to anyone who visits. It can be a museum, carnival, treasure hunt, a trip through time three stories high. For sure at Joe Ley's everything old is new again.

This place is an architect's and builder's dream. Regardless of what you need in the way of restoration or something old, there's a chance, and a good one, that you can find it in this old three-story, 1890 Hiram Roberts School.

Two acres of "wonderful stuff" provides an array of unconditional shopping. You have got to see this place to believe it. Constantly changing inventory draws visitors from throughout the world, and it has even become quite popular for filming country music videos, movies and commercials.

Numerous restaurants all over the country have bought items from Joe Ley, and when you visit you'll understand why.

The inventory here is amazing: doors, hardware, hundreds of mantels, balconies, fences, gates, posts, railings, shutters, moldings, ornaments, crystal, bronze, glass, brass, chandeliers, sconces, lamps, candle sticks, carriage lamps, and coach lights.

Joe travels all over the United States literally buying up old houses and buildings just for the windows, ironwork, staircase, columns, fountains, and on and on.

Antique toys, unique signs, carousel animals, stained glass and silver are more items that appeal to those looking for the unusual.

It's common for Joe Ley's to be written up in national publications like *House Beautiful* and *Travel and Leisure*.

This is even a good rainy day place to visit.

This remake of a more-than-twenty year old video expounding the virtues of Kentucky's history, people, culture, traditions, and even the economy is now showing!

It could easily have been called The Show of Shows, it's that fantastic.

The half hour production consists of more than 1,000 images and more than 120 interviews, and is shown in the new theater in the Kentucky Center.

Technology in the beginning is as impressive as the show, but only for a bit when the dark shades automatically lower to cover the windows and delete the light in the theater. The 100-seat five rows of chairs offer, as you would expect, unobstructed views of the 9-foot-wide-by-25-foot-

high screen. To further emphasize the technology part, a little over half-way through, the screen widens to a spectacular 45 feet.

Not only are the digital visuals impressive, but so, too, is the soundtrack. There's music, lots of it. Country, religious, orchestras, traditional and bluegrass. If it has been played in Kentucky there's a good chance it is reflected in Kentucky Show.

Those in charge of the productions will say that Kentucky Show is more than just entertainment. They'll tell you it's also there to educate and even inspire. One thing for sure after viewing this show, all of those negative stereotypes of Kentucky seem to just melt away.

The show is powerful, beginning with Kentucky as a hunting ground that attracted the likes of Daniel Boone, to division during the Civil War, to the diverse geography from the wetlands to the mountains. It is important to note that every part of Kentucky is included in this rapid-fire presentation.

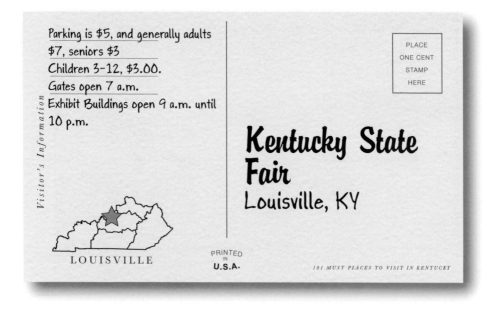

Parking is $5, and generally adults $7, seniors $3

Children 3–12, $3.00.

Gates open 7 a.m.

Exhibit Buildings open 9 a.m. until 10 p.m.

PLACE
ONE CENT
STAMP
HERE

Kentucky State Fair
Louisville, KY

LOUISVILLE

PRINTED
IN
U.S.A.

101 MUST PLACES TO VISIT IN KENTUCKY

Hundreds of thousands of people attend the Kentucky State Fair at the Kentucky Exposition Center each August.

It's one of those events where there really is something for everyone.

A state fair in Kentucky has been going on since 1902, but not always in Louisville.

The first was at Churchill Downs and promoted by a livestock association. Then the following year it moved to Owensboro. It skipped a

year before moving to Lexington in 1905. After that, Louisville became the permanent site, this time in the Parkland neighborhood of western Louisville.

In the early years the main focus was on agriculture and animal exhibits.

The modern era of the Kentucky State Fair began in 1956 when it moved to its current location, often referred to as The Fairgrounds.

The gigantic buildings that include exhibition halls, sports arenas and ample parking provide for a wide range of things to see and do, regardless of the weather outside.

Concerts featuring some of the biggest names in entertainment are center stage. So is the World's Championship Horse Show. A midway that offers over 30 rides, food vendors galore, free music events, beauty pageants, animal and bird exhibits, culinary competition, rooster crowing, and ugly lamp contests are just a few of the things that can be seen and done throughout the 10 days of the fair.

Hundreds of giveaways, free back and foot massages, lots of benches to sit on, and great people watching make the Kentucky State Fair a "must place to visit."

For sure the fair doesn't have to cost a bundle.

Louisville Slugger Museum
Louisville, KY

The Louisville Slugger baseball bat, over the years, has become one of the best known icons in all of America.

The company began making bats as a secondary line, back in 1884, and today the Hillerich & Bradsby Company has its product in virtually every Little League through Major League ballparks in the country.

Today in downtown Louisville the H & B has combined its factory with a museum, and in doing so has become a major "must see" attraction.

Although the company's headquarters have always been in Louisville, for a few years bat production was done across the river in Jeffersonville, Indiana. However, in 1996 Hillerich & Bradsby returned the operation back to Louisville, and into a new headquarter at 800 West Main Street.

Don't worry you won't have a problem finding the museum. Leaning against the five story building is the world's largest baseball bat. It stands 120-feet tall, weights 34 tons and is made of hollow carbon steel that simulates the wooden bat used by Babe Ruth in the 1920s.

On the inside, the story of baseball is told, and particularly the art of hitting.

Louisville Slugger Museum has just completed a major updating, and now offers visitors a chance to stand in the batters box and swing bats used by Mickey Mantle, Rod Carew, David Ortiz, and other stars. Ruth's bat with 21 notches indicating 21 home runs he hit in 1927.

One of the most prized exhibits is a bat used by Joe DiMaggio. Never before on public display, the bat fetched a whopping $340,000 at auction a few years back.

There's also a children's area that offers baseball themed crafts, and puzzles, as well as a T-ball batting cage.

One very popular display is the Forest to Factory that shows the evolution of a tree into a finely crafted baseball bat.

Factory tours are a mainstay of the museum.

1100 Trevillian Way
Phone: 502/459-2181
Open: 10 a.m.-4 p.m.,
September-February
10 a.m.-5 p.m.,
March-Labor Day
Admission: Adults $11.95;
Children 3 to 11, $8.50; 2 and
under FREE; Seniors $9.95

Visitor's Information

Louisville Zoo
Louisville, KY

PLACE
ONE CENT
STAMP
HERE

LOUISVILLE

PRINTED
IN
U.S.A.

101 MUST PLACES TO VISIT IN KENTUCKY

W ho doesn't enjoy a visit to the zoo? Often overlooked across Kentucky, the Louisville Zoo is a major attraction that in spite of its nearly one million visitors a year often doesn't receive the notoriety it deserves.

This 135-acre attraction is a real big-time zoo, exhibiting elephants, lions, tigers, gorillas, giraffes, zebras, orangutans, gazelles, and on and on.

Since 1969, when the zoo opened, it has gone through an ongoing evolution that has made it one of the premier venues in this area of the

United States. Today it has more than 1,300 exotic animals.

The Louisville Zoo has earned the distinction of featuring the first exhibit in the world to use a system of rotating a variety of animals into one exhibit. Called "Islands," this exhibit permits animals to explore different habitats throughout a given day, as if they were in the wild. Furthermore, the exhibit is the first to have natural predator and prey in the same space.

Visitors can purchase what is called a "Zoo Key." It is in the shape of one of the animals, and throughout the zoo the key can be inserted into the designated "Zoo Key" boxes and in turn a song is played or information announced about this particular animal.

As the Louisville Zoo continues its quest to become even better, a major construction project called Glacier Run is nearing completion. It is the first new major attraction since the Gorilla Forest that opened in 2002.

Glacier Run is a multi-million dollar exhibit that will include a 140,000 gallon pool for seals and sea lions, and an 85,000 gallon-pool for polar bears.

Glacier Run will mirror a small Artic town that allows animals of the wild to stroll through the towns in glass-enclosed corridors.

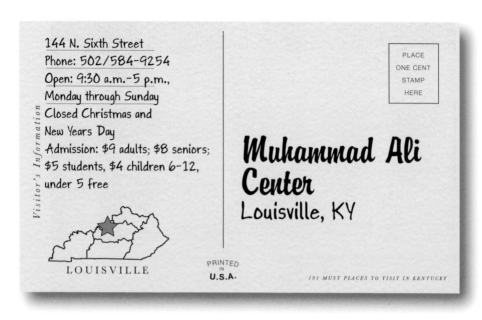

144 N. Sixth Street
Phone: 502/584-9254
Open: 9:30 a.m.-5 p.m.,
Monday through Sunday
Closed Christmas and
New Years Day
Admission: $9 adults; $8 seniors;
$5 students, $4 children 6-12,
under 5 free

Visitor's Information

LOUISVILLE

PRINTED
IN
U.S.A.

Muhammad Ali Center
Louisville, KY

101 MUST PLACES TO VISIT IN KENTUCKY

O pened in 2005, this 94,000 square-foot museum, dedicated to perhaps the most recognizable name in the world, pays tribute to the man whose life began as Cassius Clay in Louisville.

The Muhammad Ali Center's multiple levels are full of first class, award-winning exhibits. From the 16-foot by 16-foot boxing ring that was used in the movie *Ali*, to the replacement Olympic Gold Medal from his 1960 Olympics in Rome, to his 1978 Rolls-Royce, to the special

Tibetan Mandala given to him by the Dalai Lama, the Center presents Ali's life in the most accurate of forms. One area includes a recorded boxing segment in the interactive Train with Ali that was recorded by his daughter Laila Ali.

His life is portrayed with the positives as well as the negatives, and this takes in what was true and what was perceived.

Ali images throughout his life that revisit his youth of brashness, tell anyone who cared to listen, how pretty and great he was. He wasn't called the Louisville Lip just because he could box.

The Ali Center offers 2½ levels of exhibits, educational and public programming, an auditorium, several classrooms, the Howard L. Bingham Gallery, the LeRoy Neiman Gallery, a library and archives, meeting and event space, a retail shop and café.

Ali's life was much more than that of a boxer and this Center aggressively points this out.

Don't expect to see just boxing memorabilia here. The more-than-40 interactive exhibits, incorporating 19 different languages, with many geared toward children, offers something for everyone.

One of the Center's goals is to spiritually bring individuals together in a cultural setting, and it has accomplished that.

This is a world class event that probably flies under the radar screen for most Kentuckians, unless their interest is agricultural. Yes, Kentucky is still considered an ag state by most standards, but the National Farm Machinery Show is more than just agricultural.

It's entertainment! It's innovative technology. It's fun!

This super-sized show has taken place each February at the Kentucky Exposition Center for some 45 years, and it just keeps getting better. With over 1.2 million square feet of exhibit space, families can browse, shop, eat and be dazzled by everything that goes on here. There are some 800 exhibits under one roof, and it is simply amazing to see what the future has in store for computers, electronics, dairy equipment, irrigation systems, mowers, tools, tillers, and, of course, tractors, trucks and trailers.

Even if you had to pay to see this show it would be well worth it. But admission is free and so are many of the seminars.

There is an admission fee, however, to the Championship Tractor Pull that is held in con-

junction with National Farm Machinery Show.

Held inside Freedom Hall next door, this event might be slightly misnamed. This super-charged competition is the nation's oldest indoor tractor pull, and also includes trucks of all shapes and sizes. Talk about horsepower. These are some of the best and most powerful in the world. There's four evenings of "pulling." You'll want to check ahead for ticket prices. Oh yes, you may want to take some ear plugs with you for this.

Space is also available for RV parking with hookups. There is a charge.

This nationally renowned art show in old Louisville has come a long way baby!

From somewhat of a meager beginning when maybe a street and several sidewalks were blocked so some of the locals could display their artistic crafts, this festival has grown into a mega event.

Crowds today for the three-day event have been estimated at 300,000 people, and blocks and blocks of street space is now included. There are so many people who attend that shuttle to and from outside parking venues are a necessity.

The quality of merchandise displayed by the more-than-750 artist and artisans is generally of high grade. For sure it is no flea market.

You name it and it is here: jewelry, pictures, frames, Christmas ornaments, clothing, stained glass, scarves and carvings.

As entertaining and fun the art show itself is, the real enjoyment for many is the opportunity to see the beautiful old homes of Louisville. It's the same ones F. Scott Fitzgerald alluded to in some of his writings. The Victorian architecture of these gigantic homes, some with fort-like turrets, with only a few feet separating them, offers a treasured glimpse into what Louisville was like before the suburbs.

For sure you'll want to wear comfortable shoes, and one of those light-weight fold up carrying carts with wheels might come in handy. If nothing else, you can flip it over and sit on it to rest awhile.

Trinity High School
4011 Shelbyville Road
Tickets: Phone 502/895-9427

Saint X High School
1609 Poplar Level Road
Tickets: Phone 502/637-4712

PLACE
ONE CENT
STAMP
HERE

St. X-Trinity
Football Game
Louisville, KY

LOUISVILLE

PRINTED
IN
U.S.A.

101 MUST PLACES TO VISIT IN KENTUCKY

Kentucky may be considered a basketball state, but there's a time when just about everybody in the state stops to see who wins a high school football game.

On the fourth Friday night in September, a pair of high school football powerhouses, St. Xavier and Trinity, square off in a rivalry that dates back to 1956. The game is so big that it is played in Papa John's Cardinal Stadium on the campus of the University of Louisville.

Year in and year out this is Friday night football at its best.

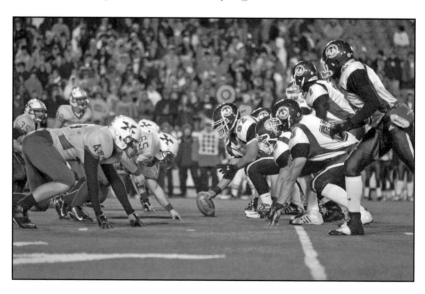

St. X and Trinity are both annually ranked among the best prep football teams in the nation, and over the years, many of their graduates have gone on to play at the collegiate level as well as in the National Football League.

But on this night in September in Louisville it's all about high school football, with usually the winner going on to a state championship.

What makes this game so special is that its draw is so far reaching. Typically more than 35,000 fans are in attendance, many of which have no connection to either school. They are there just to see great football. Alumni from both schools come out of the woodwork to party, tailgate and cheer for their teams, but the St. X-Trinity game now attracts more than just the locals. Recently a national sports network featured the game as one of the great rivalry sporting events in the country.

As of 2008, the St. X Tigers led the Trinity Shamrocks 34-31-2. This includes regular season and state play-off games.

500 Fourth Avenue
(corner of 4th& Walnut)
Phone: 502/585-3200 or
800/333-3399

Visitor's Information

Seelbach Hotel
Louisville, KY

LOUISVILLE

PRINTED
IN
U.S.A.

101 MUST PLACES TO VISIT IN KENTUCKY

There's probably not another hotel in all of Kentucky with such a storied history as the Seelbach Hotel.

From the time it opened in 1905 at the unheard cost of $950,000 in Louisville's downtown at the corner of Fourth and Walnut, the Seelbach has always been viewed as one of the most luxurious hotels around.

Over the years the hotel, built by German immigrant brothers, Louis and Otto Seelbach, hosted movie stars, governors, nine U.S. Presidents and even the infamous gangster Al Capone. Novelist F. Scott Fitzgerald,

an occasional guest at the hotel, even used the Seelbach as a backdrop for Tom and Daisy Buchanan's wedding in "The Great Gatsby."

Although the hotel underwent expansions and renovations throughout its history, as new luxury hotels began to be built in the suburb, the Seelbach was forced to close its doors in 1975. It stayed closed for seven years before reopening in 1982. A year later the property was one of only 40 hotels worldwide to be selected by the prestigious Preferred Hotels Association.

Today the Seelbach is under the Hilton flag, and its famous Oakroom restaurant is a AAA Five Diamond Award winner, the highest of honors. Its elegant southern hospitality is further accented by turn-of-the century antiques and art, while at the same time bringing forward modern amenities and state-of-the art technology.

To see this grand hotel and all of its Gatsby-style elegance, standing as it was intended when built by the Seelbach brothers some 105 years ago, is a testimonial to not only Louisville, but Kentucky as well.

As a city landmark listed on the National Register of Historic Places, this hotel and its entire ambiance is well worth a visit even if you don't spend the night.

2035 South Third Street
Phone: 502/634-2700
Open: Gallery Hours: 10:30 a.m.-
4 p.m., Tue, Wed and Fri
10:30 a.m.-8 p.m., Thursday;
10:30 a.m.-5 p.m., Saturday;
12-5 p.m. Sunday
Closed on Monday
Admission: Free
Website: www.speedmuseum.org

Visitor's Information

Speed Art Museum
Louisville, KY

LOUISVILLE

PRINTED
IN
U.S.A.

101 MUST PLACES TO VISIT IN KENTUCKY

D on't be misled by the name. It has nothing to do with pictures of fast cars. Instead it was the name of the family who founded it.

The permanent collection of the J.B. Speed Art Museum spans 6,000 years of human creativity, and is the largest and oldest such museum in Kentucky.

The Museum has distinguished collections of 17th and 18th century art, as well as significant contemporary American paintings and sculptures.

Established in 1927, and housing more than 12,000 pieces in its

permanent collection, the Speed Museum presents a world-class assortment of ancient Egyptian, Dutch, Flemish, French and contemporary art.

The Museum exhibits Renaissance and Baroque tapestries, as well as African and Native American works.

Visitors can also expect to see much more than a global influence. Kentucky displays of paintings, sculpture, and even furniture are prominent, so it was only fitting when historian Thomas D. Clark listed the Speed Art Museum as a "Kentucky Treasure."

Sometime art museums take on a "stuffy-feel," but not here. There is as much sophistication as a visitor wants. But the museum also encourages the entire family to enjoy the experience. A hands-on gallery, featuring 30 activities, multi-media, and works of art are there for all ages to enjoy.

In 1997, the Speed Art Museum underwent a $12 million expansion and renovation, thus allowing for the facilitation of major exhibitions of photography, painting, and sculpture.

More than 180,000 visit the museum annually, located near the University of Louisville's Belknap Campus. A café and gift shop encourages visitors to stay awhile.

The hours of operation are a bit confusing, so pay close attention.

Greater Louisville Convention &
Visitors Bureau
Phone: 888/LOUISVILLE

PLACE
ONE CENT
STAMP
HERE

Visitor's Information

Thunder Over Louisville
Louisville, KY

LOUISVILLE

PRINTED
IN
U.S.A.

101 MUST PLACES TO VISIT IN KENTUCKY

What started as a good fireworks show in a football stadium has turned into something now considered one of the top 100 events in North America.

Thunder Over Louisville annually jump starts the two week long celebration of the Kentucky Derby Festival on the river front in downtown Louisville.

In 1990, the Derby Festival had a ceremonial kick-off at old Cardinal Stadium, but the following year moved it to the river. From several thousand to now close to a million spectators see this awesome show that rates as the largest annual fireworks show in the nation and top five air shows.

Early on, there were a few aerobatic acts and a sky diving team. Now Thunder, in the day-long event showcases more than 100 planes, several aerobatic units and sky diving teams.

136

The hundred of thousands of people who line both the Kentucky and Indiana sides of the Ohio River, see not only the spectacular air show, but also a Zambelli pyrotechnics display. The fast paced, 28-minute show originates from eight 400-foot barges assembled on both sides of 2nd Street Bridge. The barges act as the stages from which the fireworks blast-off.

Fortunately fireworks can be shot during rain, and because of this Thunder Over Louisville has never been cancelled.

Waterfront Park is open for free public viewing, but this show is so massive that it can be seen from almost anywhere in the area.

As might be expected, Kentucky Aprils are, weather-wise, unpredictable. High temperatures have ranged from the mid-40s to mid-80s.

More than 2,000 people are involved in the production of Thunder Over Louisville. The day normally gets underway at 3 p.m. with the air show, followed at 9:30 p.m. with the fireworks.

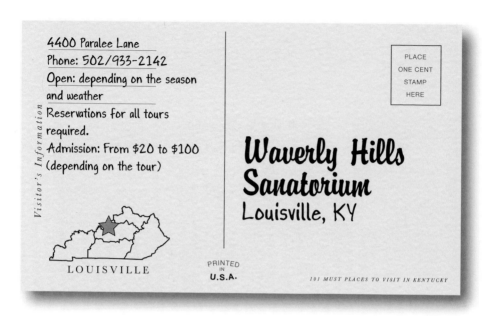

4400 Paralee Lane
Phone: 502/933-2142
Open: depending on the season and weather
Reservations for all tours required.
Admission: From $20 to $100 (depending on the tour)

Visitor's Information

LOUISVILLE

PRINTED
IN
U.S.A.

PLACE
ONE CENT
STAMP
HERE

Waverly Hills Sanatorium
Louisville, KY

101 MUST PLACES TO VISIT IN KENTUCKY

Thank goodness this old place has been saved. There were probably enough reasons, mainly disrepair, to tear the old hospital down that sits atop Waverly Hills, on 600 acres that is said to be the highest point in Louisville.

Charlie and Tina Mattingly, however stepped up and set about to make this former 500 bed tuberculosis hospital a tourist attraction.

In early 1900 tuberculosis was a serious, deadly disease. Those carrying the illness were often isolated from the general public in a facility where they could rest and have lots of fresh air.

Waverly Hills near Pleasure Ridge Park was the perfect location. Construction on the huge hospital began in 1924 and completed in 1926. It could accommodate over 500 patients and was said to be the most modern and well equipped hospital of its kind in the nation.

For the next 35 years it operated as a T.B. hospital before closing in 1961. A year later, after being quarantined and renovated, it re-opened as Wood Haven Medical Services. It closed in 1980, and at one time the campus-like setting included seven buildings.

Today Waverly Hills Sanatorium is open for tours and even overnight stays. Over the last few years the property has gained a reputation for being inhabited by spirits. Paranormal investigators from throughout the country visit the old hospital with their various ghost-hunting equipment in search of the unexplainable happenings here.

Waverly Hills is reported to be one of the most haunted places in the world, so one of several tours just might be to your liking.

For unknown reasons lights go on and off, doors open and close, and colored lights that appear unexplainably move up and down the halls.

Visitors are encouraged to call ahead for reservations and tour schedules. There are options for a two, four, and eight hour visit. The four hour is considered a half-night, while the eight hour is a full overnight.

Historic tours of the old hospital are given once a month on Sundays at 2:30 p.m.

Are you brave enough?

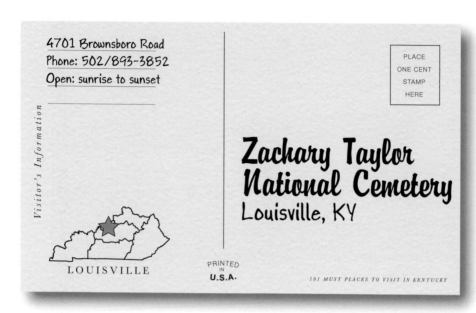

Visitor's Information

Zachary Taylor National Cemetery
Louisville, KY

LOUISVILLE

PRINTED
IN
U.S.A.

101 MUST PLACES TO VISIT IN KENTUCKY

It would be a safe to say that the average Kentuckian may not realize that the twelfth President of the United States is buried in Kentucky.

Zachary Taylor Cemetery, in northeast Louisville is where the former President, and his first lady Margaret, are buried.

Taylor had been a decorated war hero of the Mexican-American War, and even before that, won fame as an "Indian fighter on the new frontier." Because of his heroics he was known as "old rough and ready."

By 1848 his popularity led the Whig Party to nominate him for the presidency of the United States. Taylor won the election that November, but after attending a celebration on July 4, 1850, in Washington, D.C., he became ill and died five days later.

To this day there was never an exact cause to his sickness. Some said cholera, others said typhoid fever, while there was even a group that speculated he was poisoned.

More than 10,000 people lined the funeral route to see the President laid to rest.

Initially Taylor was buried at the Congressional Cemetery in Washington, but in November 1850, he was brought to the site in Kentucky that had been part of his father's 400-acre estate.

Zachary Taylor Cemetery is one of seven national cemeteries in the state.

In 1883, the state of Kentucky erected a 50-foot monument near Taylor's grave and topped it with a life-size statue of him, and in 1928, an act of Congress established the grounds as a National Cemetery.

Those who visit the former President's burial site will see a mausoleum in which he and his wife are interred.

Beech Bend Park	Bowling Green, Ky
Kentucky Down Under	Horse Cave, Ky
Kentucky's Stonehenge	Munfordville, Ky
Lake Cumberland	South Central Ky
Lost River Cave & Valley	Bowling Green, Ky
Mammoth Cave National Park	Mammoth Cave, Ky
National Corvette Museum	Bowling Green, Ky
Russellville, Kentucky	Russellville, Ky
Wigwam Village	Cave City, Ky

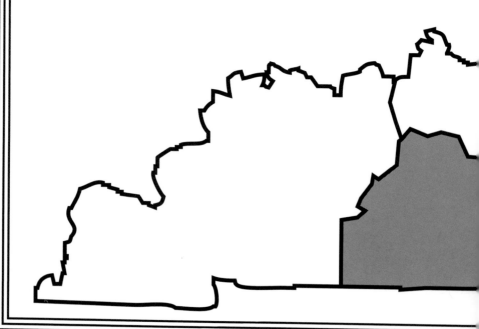

South Central Region

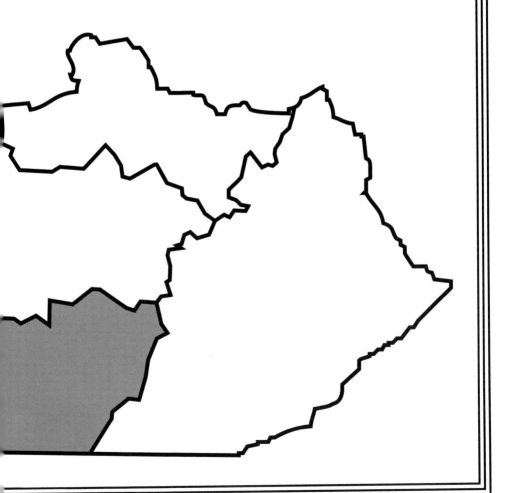

798 Beech Bend Road
Phone: 270/781-7634
Open: Daily, Memorial Day to
mid-August; weekends only
May and September, Sunday 11
a.m.-7 p.m., Monday-Friday, 10
a.m.-7 p.m., Saturday, 10 a.m.-
8 p.m.

Visitor's Information

PLACE
ONE CENT
STAMP
HERE

Beech Bend Park
Bowling Green, KY

SOUTH CENTRAL

PRINTED
IN
U.S.A.

101 MUST PLACES TO VISIT IN KENTUCKY

S ince the late 1800s people have been going to the grove of Beech trees in the bend of the Barren River just outside of Bowling Green. Of course this was long before it became an amusement park, but nevertheless it was a beautiful place for the locals to gather to picnic, play games and just enjoy watching the river flow past.

A summer was not complete unless it included several trips to the site.

Today that site is Beech Bend Park, a 325-acre amusement park, raceway and campground.

What Charlie Garvin started back in 1942 when he bought the property, Dallas Jones and his family have taken it to another level.

Beech Bend is a classic.

Considered perhaps the best, family owned amusement park in the south, it has more than 40 rides, including the most twisted wooden roller coaster throughout seven states.

The Kentucky Rumbler is a $4.4 million coaster

that reaches a speed of 57 miles per hour and whirls around a 73 degree bank. It took more than 240,000 linear feet of pressure-treated yellow pine to build the structure that covers a length of over 2,800 feet.

Beech Bend also includes a Splash Lagoon, giant swimming pool and Wild Mouse Ride.

Truly, this is one of the legendary little amusement parks in the nation.

The adjacent raceway drag strip plays host to some of the biggest automotive and motorcycle events in the country.

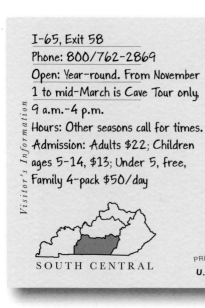

I-65, Exit 58

Phone: 800/762-2869

Open: Year-round. From November
1 to mid-March is Cave Tour only,
9 a.m.-4 p.m.

Hours: Other seasons call for times.

Admission: Adults $22; Children
ages 5-14, $13; Under 5, free,
Family 4-pack $50/day

Visitor's Information

PLACE
ONE CENT
STAMP
HERE

Kentucky Down Under

Horse Cave, KY

SOUTH CENTRAL

PRINTED
IN
U.S.A.

101 MUST PLACES TO VISIT IN KENTUCKY

Kentucky Down Under, by its mere name is supposed to bring a bit of Australian and its outback to Kentucky.

And it does!

Without question this is a first rate family attraction for just about any age children and adults. You'll want to allow several hours here.

It can start just about any place you want it to, but how about the Outback Walkabout? Kangaroos, Emus, and Wallabies are there for a hands-on experience.

Children won't want to leave the gigantic bird cage. Full of exotic feathered friends, the cage allows people to interact and even hand-feed many of them.

And then there's the Discovery Area, turtles, snakes, blue-tongued skinks, and bearded dragons make for quite an experience regardless of age.

Camp Carroboree teaches the process of throwing a boomerang, or even learning to play a didgeridoo. You might even find out what cooroboree means.

Some people like to take a break from the above ground fun and go down into one of the most beautiful show caves anywhere on earth. Kentucky Caverns, with its constant 55 degree temperature, can, especially during the summer, provide a cool, refreshing diversion, while at the same time displaying almost unbelievable underground rock formations. The cave tour is approximately 45 minutes.

Many of those who have been to Kentucky Down Under previously, enjoy returning to one of the most popular venues, The Woolshed. To feed the baby lambs, or milk a cow, or even sheer a sheep is part of an experience not soon forgotten. But neither will be impressive exhibitions of border collies rounding up a herd of sheep in a field and then "directing" them into a pen.

One block off Main Street
Phone: 270/524-4752-
888/686-3673
Admission: FREE

Visitor's Information

PLACE
ONE CENT
STAMP
HERE

Kentucky's
Stonehenge
Munfordville, KY

SOUTH CENTRAL

PRINTED
IN
U.S.A.

101 MUST PLACES TO VISIT IN KENTUCKY

A former mayor of Munfordville's obsession with collecting very large rocks has turned into a tourist attraction for this little town that sits on the banks of the Green River, and is known more for its Civil War history than anything else.

Move over Civil War and make room for Chester Fryer's recreation of England's Stonehenge. Although Kentucky's Stonehenge does not exactly follow the layout of the real one, it is close in many ways.

"There are some similarities," says the former mayor, "but I constructed mine to reflect points on a compass."

Other rocks mark the cardinal directions in Fryer's masterpiece.

One of the most unusual elements of his rock creation is that it sits on the same property as his home. And although Fryer is proud of his Stonehenge, he likes to point out all of the other rock and stone creations he has assembled over his several acres of grounds.

He's even broken his displays into categories: Earth Mysteries, The Garden of Gethsemane, Rock Gardens, and Rock Park. Some of his formations have been made to look like Civil War cannons.

Although England's Stonehenge dates back to 3,000 B.C., with burials being a major component of the mysterious stone formations, the Kentucky attraction sits there just for people to enjoy.

The question of "why" begs to be answered.

"Why not"? Fryer says. "I like to work with big rocks and it has become just a hobby. I'm glad people like to look at them."

The actual building and purpose of England's Stonehenge remain a mystery that has long drawn speculation from many sources. This is certainly not the case with Kentucky's Stonehenge.

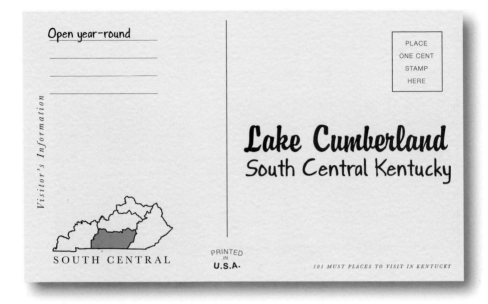

Visitor's Information

Lake Cumberland
South Central Kentucky

SOUTH CENTRAL

PRINTED
IN
U.S.A.

101 MUST PLACES TO VISIT IN KENTUCKY

Those who own businesses around Lake Cumberland like to refer to it as a vacationer's paradise.

The 63,000-acre lake is one of the largest man-made bodies of water east of the Mississippi River, with an average depth of 90 feet, and it touches about 1,300 miles of shoreline.

When the Cumberland River was damned up some 60 years ago, there were only a handful of people who could have envisioned what

Lake Cumberland would one day financially mean to this region of Kentucky.

Tourism flourishes in the several counties that surround the lake, considered to be one of the most beautiful in this part of the United States.

The Lake Cumberland area has gained a national reputation for houseboats, not only for actually enjoying them but manufacturing. Labeled "houseboat capital of the world," there are houseboat builders in at least five nearby counties. These boats are then floated or transported to other lakes throughout Kentucky or the United States.

Towns like Somerset, Monticello, Russell Springs, Columbia and Albany have factories open for visitors to visit.

But Lake Cumberland is much more than houseboats.

Fishing is said to be fantastic. And the scenic vistas offer outstanding photo opportunities. Hundreds of rental cottages and cabins surround the lake, and for those who want to go a little more upscale, Lake Cumberland State Resort Park at Jamestown may be to your liking.

Of course each town near the lake has lodging, restaurants, campgrounds, marinas and everything that goes with it.

Lost River Cave & Valley

Bowling Green, Ky

SOUTH CENTRAL

PRINTED IN U.S.A.

101 MUST PLACES TO VISIT IN KENTUCKY

Beginning in the 1930s and continuing into the 60s this geological phenomenon was operated as an underground night club. The glory days of Lost River Cave hosted big band sounds of the NBC Orchestra and stars like singer Dinah Shore. It was a great place to beat the heat on a hot summer night and have fun in the cave's cool 57 degree natural air conditioning.

Long before that, however, Lost River Cave and Valley was occupied by human life as far back as 6,000 B.C. In 1825, Warren County's first flour mill was built just above the cave on what today is U.S. 31-W highway, and from 1861 to 1863, Union and Confederate soldiers occupied the area, as many as 40,000 at one time. And after robbing a bank in nearby Russellville, Kentucky, Jesse James and his gang found the cave to be a convenient place to hide.

The Valley was formed thousands of years ago with the collapse of a sizable cave system, making the more than 20 acres a most unusual and unique topographic feature. As a result, the Valley is a study

in nature. Winding hiking trails, hundreds of varieties of trees, native Kentucky wildflowers and birds, all make the moderate walk to Lost River's Butterfly Garden and water-filled Blue Holes a wonderful experience.

Lost River Valley serves as a natural drainage basin for 72 square miles. Collected water flows underground and resurfaces in four different pools in the valley. It is these pools that are referred to as Blue Holes because of the sun filtering through the trees and dancing on the water.

It is the water from the Blue Holes that flows some 300 yards on the surface only to disappear again into the mouth of the cave. Years ago *Ripley's Believe It or Not* promoted Lost River as the "shortest, deepest river in the world."

For almost a decade the cave surrendered to neglect, becoming a dumping ground for old tires, appliances, garbage and even old cars. Lost River was all but a forgotten place. But thanks to a group of volunteers it has been rediscovered.

Today, visitors can enjoy a tranquil boat ride into the cave, walk among the tree-tops over a 143-foot bridge that gently slopes into the valley's ground level, or dance the night away at many of Lost River's frequently scheduled summer dances on the gigantic dance floor.

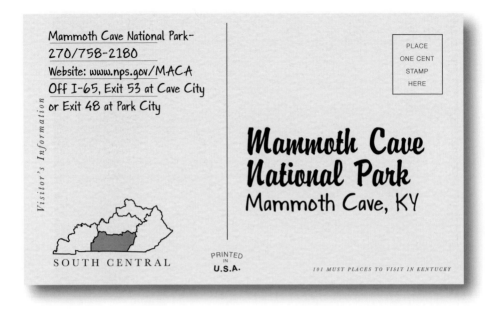

Visitor's Information

Mammoth Cave National Park–
270/758-2180
Website: www.nps.gov/MACA
Off I-65, Exit 53 at Cave City
or Exit 48 at Park City

Mammoth Cave National Park
Mammoth Cave, KY

SOUTH CENTRAL

PRINTED IN U.S.A.

101 MUST PLACES TO VISIT IN KENTUCKY

With over 360 miles of charted passageways, Mammoth Cave National Park lays claim to the largest cave infrastructure in the world.

Ever since John Houchins, an Edmonson County hunter, chased a bear into a large opening in the ground back in 1798, people have been coming to Mammoth Cave to see what the heck is down there.

Visitors to the park are often surprised to learn that it is the second oldest tourist attraction in America, following only Niagara Falls. Tour guides beginning with candles and lanterns have been taking visitors down under since 1816.

In 1926, Congress authorized the establishment of Mammoth Cave as a National Park. And then in 1981, the United Nations designated it as a World Heritage Site, in the company of the Grand Canyon and Egyptian Pyramids.

For sure, with the multitude of passageways, it is impossible to see everything in a single day. Thirteen different tours are there

for the choosing. The short tours provide a glimpse of cave environment. They vary in cost depending on the sections of the cave to be toured, the time duration, and comfort level of the passageways. In other words some are more labor intense than others.

There's a cave tour length that can fit just about any visitor's interest. A two hour trek can explore a variety of such subjects as cave archeology, prehistoric and historic exploration, geology and cave biology.

The longest tour requires four hours and covers four and one half miles. Also offered is a "Wild Cave" tour, for those who really want to get down and dirty. Headlamps are used and participants are required to crawl and climb through and over some of the less developed trails.

Mammoth Cave National Park is much more than stalagmites and stalactites. Everyone who visits Mammoth Cave doesn't have a primary interest in walking through a year-round 55 degree cave. Some come here for what's above ground, the scenic beauty of the 53,000 acre park. Camping, hiking, bicycling, bird watching, photos, and other artistic endeavors, make this visit a place for all to enjoy.

The Mammoth Cave Hotel (270/758-2225) is adjacent to the park's new Visitor Center where all of the tours begin.

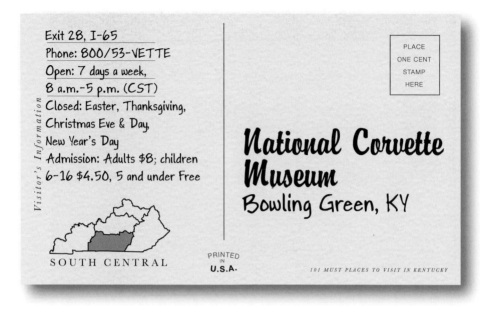

Exit 28, I-65
Phone: 800/53-VETTE
Open: 7 days a week,
8 a.m.-5 p.m. (CST)
Closed: Easter, Thanksgiving,
Christmas Eve & Day,
New Year's Day
Admission: Adults $8; children
6-16 $4.50, 5 and under Free

Visitor's Information

PLACE
ONE CENT
STAMP
HERE

National Corvette Museum
Bowling Green, KY

SOUTH CENTRAL

PRINTED
IN
U.S.A.

101 MUST PLACES TO VISIT IN KENTUCKY

The National Corvette Museum is a world-class automobile museum dedicated to what is called "America's Sports Car." The added value of a visit here is that adjacent to the Museum sits the Corvette Assembly Plant that is also open for tours (270/745-8019).

You may not realize that every Corvette made is produced in Bowling Green, so it's only fitting that visitors can see these beautiful cars under one roof.

The Corvette was first introduced in 1953, and over the years its evolution has continued to remain a part of Americana.

This spectacular facility opened in 1994, and with its recent 47,000 square foot addition, now puts the rarest of Corvettes in a 100,000 plus square foot setting.

The "you can't miss it," 11 story-tall Skydome overlooks this sprawling venue, and inside is close to 100 dream cars that rotate in and out on a regular basis in order to keep things fresh.

Upon entering the museum is the Chevrolet Theater where you'll watch as the history of the Corvette unfolds. Then it's on to see up close some very rare, one-of-a-kind classics, several race cars, and some exotic experimental cars that never reached the production line.

The Museum also has a state-of-the-art Corvette library and archives, conference center, Hall of Fame, café, and gift shop.

A unique feature here is that those who purchase Corvettes regardless of where they live can arrange to have it delivered to them in a special "ceremony," at the National Corvette Museum.

This is a museum that is fun for everyone regardless of knowledge of automobiles. Who doesn't like to look at beautiful Corvettes?

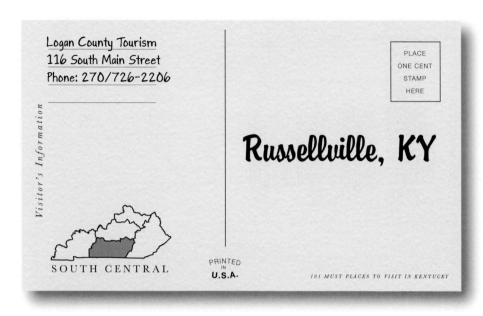

Logan County Tourism
116 South Main Street
Phone: 270/726-2206

Visitor's Information

PLACE
ONE CENT
STAMP
HERE

Russellville, KY

SOUTH CENTRAL

PRINTED
IN
U.S.A.

101 MUST PLACES TO VISIT IN KENTUCKY

It's probably safe to say in 1868 not one single Russellville resident would have thought that a bank robbery on March 20 of the same year would, over 140 years later, still be the most famous event to happen in this Logan County town.

Although Jesse James and his gang's visit were short lived, the impact it made is the hook used today when tourists and other visitors come to town.

It was the James gang's first Kentucky bank job and it netted them over $9,000 after they shot and wounded the bank's president.

The Southern Deposit Bank still stands, and today is part of the private home of a local resident.

Of course Russellville and Logan County are much more than a famous bank heist. Because of the notoriety of the James gang, there are several towns across Kentucky that wishes "ole Jesse" had robbed something in their town.

Russellville today is a blend of rural small town activities that include agricultural and industry with just the right touch of sophistication.

158

It starts with the town square. Surrounding a cast-iron fountain are numerous historical markers, as well as monuments, memorial stones and an old cannon. It's an outdoor stroll down history lane.

The residential district has some 200 homes that range from 1815 to 1940, and the town has produced four Kentucky governors, a governor each in Illinois, Texas and Florida, five U.S. Senators, six congressmen, three Kentucky chief justices, three U.S. Ambassadors, three federal Cabinet officers, and four men who died at the Alamo, among them legendary Jim Bowie.

Visitors can step inside and see the restored early 1800 Caldwell Saddle Factory, and tour the 1820 Bibb House. The son of the home's builder developed Bibb lettuce.

A downtown walking tour brochure points out 35 homes and buildings of interest.

There may not be another town in Kentucky, at least one with a population of 7,000, which has such a concentration of beautiful, historic homes as Russellville.

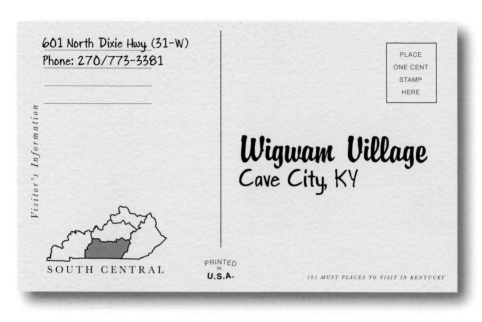

601 North Dixie Hwy (31-W)
Phone: 270/773-3381

Visitor's Information

Wigwam Village
Cave City, KY

SOUTH CENTRAL

PRINTED IN
U.S.A.

101 MUST PLACES TO VISIT IN KENTUCKY

Without question Wigwam Village is the most unusual motel in Kentucky. It has been, since Frank Redford built it in 1937.

Fourteen of the cone-shaped concrete structures make up the "village" along with an office. Arranged in a semi-circle, facing a grassy common area, the motel is listed on the National Register of Historic Places for good reason. It represents the best of retro Americana, when travelers out of the north pointed their cars out on two lane highways and headed South on vacation.

Wigwam Village, back then before the interstate roadways, competed with all of the other local roadside tourist cabins. But because of its wigwam look, it became one of the most popular and well-known over-nights in the area. It didn't hurt that it is located in the heart of cave country.

Today, Wig-wam Village is still popular, especially on weekends in the spring and summer. Many of those staying here are returning to celebrate an

anniversary, or where they honeymooned. Anyone planning to come here had better make a reservation.

This is not a five star overnight. But it is a fun place to visit and literally step back into days gone by.

Rooms are filled with a double bed, made from early 1940s hickory and cane. Air conditioning units keep you cool in the summer, and space heaters warm in the winter. The bathrooms are small, but sufficient.

Originally there were seven of the Villages scattered throughout the country, with two being in Kentucky. However, time, traffic patterns and hotel chains have taken their toll. Today, other than the Cave City location one is in Arizona, and another in California.

The big sign in front, next to the highway, reads "Sleep In a Wigwam." And though it's not one, it still may be as close as you'll get to one.

Big Bone Lick State Park	Union, Ky
Covered Bridges of Kentucky	Flemingsburg, Ky
MainStrasse Village	Covington, Ky
Maysville, Kentucky	Maysville, Ky
Newport Aquarium	Newport, Ky
The Cathedral Basilica of the Assumption	Covington, Ky

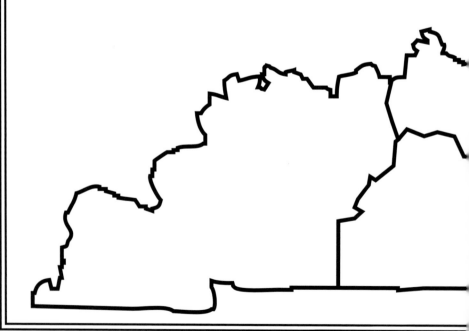

Northern Region

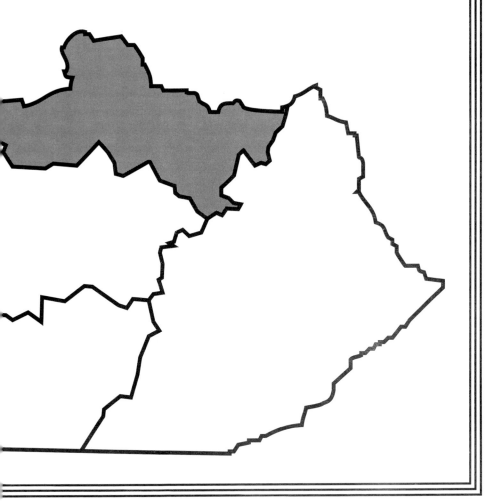

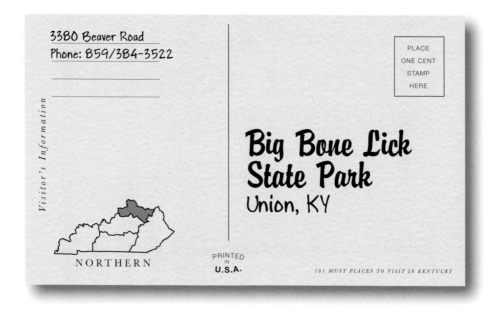

3380 Beaver Road
Phone: 859/384-3522

PLACE
ONE CENT
STAMP
HERE

Visitor's Information

Big Bone Lick State Park
Union, KY

NORTHERN

PRINTED
IN
U.S.A.

101 MUST PLACES TO VISIT IN KENTUCKY

Big Bone Lick State Park is all about history. Real history.

Here you are talking about documented history that reaches back fifteen to twenty thousand years, well before the arrival of man, much less Kentuckians.

Because of what happened in the northern Kentucky area this park has been saved by the U.S. Secretary of the Interior as a National Natural Landmark, one of only 582 in the nation.

Big Bone Lick is a member of an elite group of geological sites throughout the United States. The significance of this site is the combination that existed between the salt springs and giant mastodons, mammoths and bison.

164

For thousands of years these ancient creatures roamed through the mineral springs and swamps that are today beautiful grassy plains dotted with lots of trees, shrubs and other plant life.

Prehistoric animals would come to the salt licks and would often get stuck in the swampy land around the licks. Then they would be trampled, drowned or hunted.

Historically, as well as academically, Big Bone Lick is recognized as the birthplace of American vertebrate paleontology. Furthermore, this area played a significant role in the development of scientific research regarding extinction and the relationship of geology and paleontology throughout the world.

This National Park Service program that Big Bone Lick is now a part of began in 1962, and recognizes significant natural history sites and helps support their conservation.

The 512-acre park in southwestern Boone County is known for its unique fossil beds which date back as much as 20,000 years. The Park underwent a rigorous four-year review in order to achieve this national status.

Big Bone Lick features a bison herd, campground, museum, gift shop and a lake for bank fishing.

Covered Bridges of Kentucky
Flemingsburg, KY

NORTHERN

PRINTED
IN
U.S.A.

101 MUST PLACES TO VISIT IN KENTUCKY

A t one time there were some 400 covered bridges in Kentucky, but due to floods, fires, Mother Nature, and modernization, only thirteen remain.

Those that have survived are without question considered historic relics, and for some reason they are all located primarily in the northeastern part of the state.

Covered bridges were first built in Kentucky in the 1790s, and the justification for covering them was primarily to keep the main timbers dry and protected from the weather.

Like many things constructed, then and now, each builder had his own architectural style, some being quite simple while others a bit more complex. Regardless, they filled an important place in early day travel before the automobile came on the scene.

Fleming County is considered the State Covered Bridge Capital of Kentucky, and was so recognized in 1998. Today, three of the bridges can be seen in the county.

The length of the bridges varied in size. Whatever it took to cross a certain area was what was built. It is interesting to note that at one time the longest covered bridge in the world was in Pendleton County. It crossed the Licking River and spanned 456 feet. Built in 1871, it was damaged by flood waters in 1937 and later torn down.

The Civil War took its toll on many of the bridges, as they were torched by both Union and Confederate troops.

The state of Kentucky realizes the historic value of these covered bridges, and in recent years has done its part in repairing and rebuilding some of them.

Other counties where the bridges can be seen are Greenup, Lewis, Robertson, Bracken, Bourbon, Franklin, Washington, and Mason.

MainStrasse Village Association
406 West 6th Street
Phone: 859/491-0458

Visitor's Information

MainStrasse Village
Covington, KY

NORTHERN

PRINTED
IN
U.S.A.

101 MUST PLACES TO VISIT IN KENTUCKY

Staying true to its German influence this six block downtown area of Covington has become a tourist destination as well as a fun place for the locals to hang out.

MainStrasse Village, organized in 1879, is a collection of unique shops, restaurants and pubs, in a setting of neighborhood parks and Victorian and Italianate houses built in the mid to late 1800s. It's easy to see why MainStrasse is listed on the National Register of Historic Places.

For almost a century and a half this Main Street area of Covington (the German word for street is strasse) has been a place associated with fun and good times. In fact, in 1932 the area was annexed by the City of Covington and used as a recreational area for the circus when it came to town.

It seems that MainStrasse

168

always has something going on in addition to its daily happenings. Festivals and events like their annual Mardi Gras, Maifest, Goettafest, and hugely successful Oktoberfest draw visitors from throughout Kentucky and the Cincinnati area just across the Ohio River.

At the western end of MainStrasse Village sits the glockenspiel Carroll Chimes Bell Tower. Visitors gather here to hear the hourly 43-bell sounds from this German Gothic structure.

Another popular attraction, closer to the center of the Village, is the Goose Girl Fountain. At one time, farmers in the area raised geese, and the fountain depicts the German Grimm's fairy tale, "the Goose Girl," as a tribute to the culture of the area.

The beautiful restoration of the Village combined with cobblestone walkways, a tree-lined promenade, and informational historic markers, make for an enjoyable stroll for many of the more than 500,000 visitors annually.

Plan on spending some time here. Perhaps the toughest decision a visitor faces is what to do first and where to eat.

With 20 shops, 11 restaurants, six pubs, four saloons, a bed and breakfast and a coffee house, the choices are many.

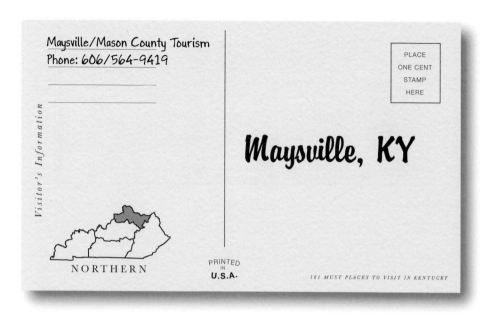

Maysville/Mason County Tourism
Phone: 606/564-9419

Visitor's Information

Maysville, KY

NORTHERN

PRINTED
IN
U.S.A.

101 MUST PLACES TO VISIT IN KENTUCKY

Maysville is an old river town for sure. Its early day houses were built on a hillside somewhat removed from the river, but with a view to die for. In earlier times commercial and passenger steamboats created lots of excitement in town around the turn of the century. The hustle and bustle at Maysville's river landings all added to the town's growth, albeit not enough to keep up with the much larger nearby city of Cincinnati.

Today, what's not to like about this charming place that sits overlooking the Ohio River in northern Kentucky?

That early day river excitement has given way to barges, tug boats, a few pleasure crafts, and an occasional visit from the paddlewheel *Delta Queen*. This, of course, doesn't mean the Ohio River is not still important. Maysville is what it is because of the river.

Old historic downtown buildings that were once boarded up have now come to life with architecturally significant face lifts. A defining moment for downtown

170

occurred several years ago with the opening of the French Quarter Inn on the river. The rooms face the river, and offer a beautiful night time view of the Simon Kenton Bridge that crosses into Ohio and the small town of Aberdeen.

Maysville is dotted with small shops of all kinds, and some of the town's brick covered side streets let you imagine how it once was when horse-drawn buggies and wagons scurried to meet the riverboats to pick up passengers and supplies.

The Rosemary Clooney Museum pays tribute to the legendary singer/movie star that went from this small town to Hollywood, but never forgot where she came from. An October festival annually honors her musical contributions.

The Kentucky Gateway Museum offers a first class collection of miniatures by Kathleen Savage Browning, as well as a genealogical and historical research library.

The National Underground Railroad Museum documents Maysville's role in the abolitionist movement and the role of slavery in America with slavery artifacts, documents and memorabilia.

Nine beautiful Robert Dafford painted flood wall murals depict the town's history, and nearby is the Albert Sidney Johnson House, the childhood home of the famous Civil War Confederate General.

Just a couple of miles from the heart of downtown and removed from the river is the Washington Historic District, an authentic pioneer village of 1790s log cabin, shops and museums.

Only a handful of covered bridges remain in Kentucky today, and most of those are in the area. The adjacent counties of Fleming and Lewis have several of the relics.

Eighteen miles away is Augusta, well-worth a visit.

Visitor's Information

One Aquarium Way
Phone: 859/261-7444
Open: 365 days a year
10 a.m.-6 p.m. (extended
summer and holiday hours)
Admission: $20 adults; $13
children, ages 2-12; children
under 2 free

NORTHERN

PLACE
ONE CENT
STAMP
HERE

Newport Aquarium
Newport, KY

PRINTED
IN
U.S.A.

101 MUST PLACES TO VISIT IN KENTUCKY

Sitting on the banks of the Ohio River the Newport Aquarium has been recognized as one of the best museum's of its type in the nation.

With some 70 exhibits and 14 galleries that include more than 200 feet of seamless acrylic tunnels which allow visitors to surround themselves with numerous varieties of aquatic life from throughout the world.

The one million gallons of water in the giant aquarium is now home

to over 7,000 aquatic creatures in an almost unbelievable state-of-the-art setting. The creativeness and technology in the layout of the facility, allows for visitors to take a journey around the globe, visiting each continent, all of the oceans, and hundreds of waterways.

The walk-thru tunnels put you right in the middle of it all, with sea creatures, sharks and rays both above you and below you. You will be completely surrounded by it all.

Not only is the Newport Aquarium entertaining, but equally educational.

One of the exhibits, Shark Central, lets visitors actually touch a shark. Sleeves can be rolled up and hands dipped into a special "touch pool" filled with various sharks and rays. This interactive exhibit lets visitors use a "two-finger touch" technique in properly touching a shark or ray. The kids will love it. The purpose here is to educate everyone about the important role that sharks play in the aquatic environment.

The Frog Bog, for sure to change your way of thinking about frogs, allows children to interact.

Other exhibits include the Jellyfish Gallery, the Kingdom of Penguins, Gator Bayou, and Kids Central.

1140 Madison Avenue
Phone: 859/431-2060
Open: 10 a.m.-4 p.m.,
Monday through Saturday
Admission: FREE

The Cathedral Basilica of the Assumption
Covington, KY

NORTHERN

PRINTED
IN
U.S.A.

101 MUST PLACES TO VISIT IN KENTUCKY

This wonderful church's construction was begun in 1894 and completed in 1915. And though some say it has actually never been finished, it remains as something to see, regardless of ones faith. A visit here and you will see why this is a work of art, and an architectural monument to be treasured for centuries.

By definition a church attains the privilege of being called a basilica because of its antiquity, dignity, historical importance and significance as a worship center.

A closer look reveals that basilicas fall into two classes: major and minor. Only four are classified as major and they are all in Rome. There are 35 minor ones in the United States of which the Cathedral Basilica of the Assumption is one. Pope Pius XII elevated the St. Mary's Cathedral to the minor rank in 1953.

Covington's Basilica promotes itself as displaying the world's largest stained glass window. It measures 24 feet by 67 feet and con-

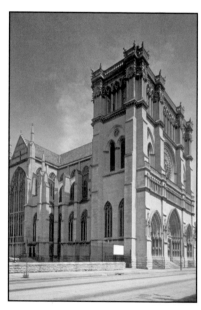

tains 117 distinctive figures. In addition there are 82 windows, all made in Munich Germany, that tell biblical stories in an art form.

Stained glass and story-telling windows have been around for centuries. Here at the Basilica the story the windows tell is just as beautiful as the art.

Historically, windows in churches filled the need of telling biblical stories to those church members who couldn't read.

The Basilica has over 70,000 visitors a year, and in 2001 it underwent a major renovation that included $1 million just for cleaning and restoration of the beautiful windows. The windows were completely taken apart, broken pieces replaced, and new lead where needed.

Directions: If you are approaching from the West, take the 12th Street exit from I-71/75. Go East on 12th street, stay on 12th through Madison Ave. Parking will be on the left behind the Cathedral. If you are approaching from the East, go south on Scott street (across the Suspension Bridge, from Ohio) through Covington. Make a right turn onto 11th Street. Parking will be on the left side of the Cathedral.

Boys State High School Basketball Tournament	Lexington, Ky
CastlePost	Lexington, Ky
Henry Clay's Home/Ashland	Lexington, Ky
Horse Farm Tours	Lexington Area
Keeneland Race Course	Lexington, Ky
Kentucky Horse Park	Lexington, Ky
Lexington Cemetery	Lexington, Ky
Man O'War's Grave	Lexington, Ky
Old Frankfort Pike	Lexington, Ky
Raven Run Nature Sanctuary	Lexington, Ky

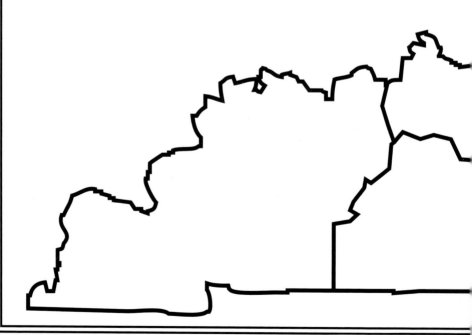

Lexington Region

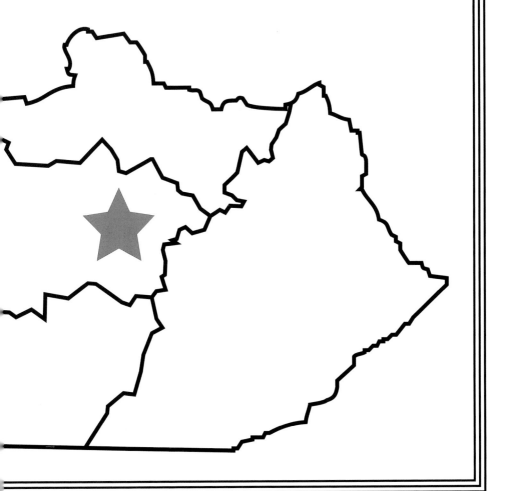

I t's promoted as "the greatest show on earth," and although that may be a stretch, the Boy's State Basketball Tournament in Kentucky is, indeed, something special.

Even if you're not a basketball purist, going to this event is uplifting. The spirit and energy of over 20,000 fans takes enthusiasm to another level.

Often referred to as "The Sweet 16," this four-day basketball tournament attracts high school teams, cheerleaders, and students from throughout the sixteen regions of Kentucky.

Played in spacious Rupp Arena in downtown Lexington, usually around the middle of March, Kentucky's boys' tournament is unique from most other states, in that it is a single tournament open to all high schools regardless of size. Many states have gone

to a class format, i.e.; Class A, Class AA, and so on. Whoever wins in Kentucky leaves little doubt as to who has the best team.

The tournament started in 1916, but hasn't always been played in Lexington. In fact, the first three were at Centre College in Danville, before moving to Lexington's U.K. Gym and then to Alumni Gym in 1924. From there it was back and forth over the years. The Armory and Freedom Hall in Louisville hosted multiple events, while Memorial Coliseum and Rupp Arena were the sites in Lexington. But in 1995 the Kentucky High School Athletic Association decided Lexington and Rupp would be the permanent venue.

The Sweet 16 is a great family event, and one of the enjoyable things is that you can have fun even if your team's not in it.

Lexington is full of good places to eat and lots of hotel rooms. However, be warned, that if you plan to go, call well ahead of time for hotel reservations.

If you live in Kentucky, you've got to go to at least one of these tournaments, if for no other reason to say you have. Kentucky is a basketball crazy state, for sure, and it all starts with this fantastic high school tournament.

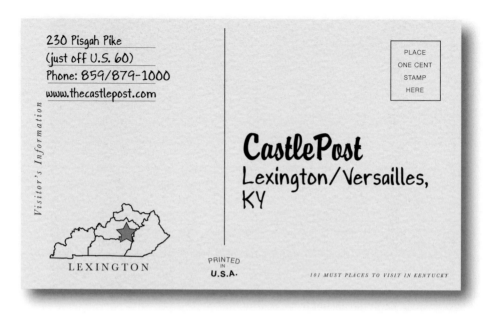

230 Pisgah Pike
(just off U.S. 60)
Phone: 859/879-1000
www.thecastlepost.com

Visitor's Information

CastlePost
Lexington/Versailles,
KY

LEXINGTON

PRINTED
IN
U.S.A.

101 MUST PLACES TO VISIT IN KENTUCKY

S uddenly it appears almost out of nowhere on U.S. 60, a stretch of road between Lexington and Versailles.

The medieval-like castle has been sitting there since 1968, causing new visitors to the area to wonder what this is all about. After all, it seems so out of place among the numerous stately horse farms that dot the bluegrass landscape surrounding it.

Four turrets anchor the corners of the massive stone wall, each reaching a height of 70 feet and even though the castle has been there for decades it had never been completed . . . until now.

Over the years there were signs indicating the property and its 53 acres was for sale. One read "No Trespassing" and another warned "Beware of Dogs."

Those signs have come down, and today the castle is open for business.

The property was purchased several years ago by Thomas Post and is now called CastlePost.

This incredible structure has 16 bedroom suites available for rent,

and hospitality rooms for private catered parties and meetings. Amenities include tennis and basketball courts, running track, pool, exercise facility, shuffle-board and Jacuzzi.

There's quite a bit of history as well as mystery about the fortress-like structure, beginning with Rex Martin and his wife Caroline. She wanted a castle built in Kentucky after vacationing in Europe. After Martin and his wife divorced in 1975, the castle was never completed.

After Post purchased the property and started renovation, a fire occurred and delayed things a bit. But now the CastlePost is certainly worth seeing, even from a distance for many. Overnights will cost $1,000 per, and prices escalate depending how much space you want and for how long.

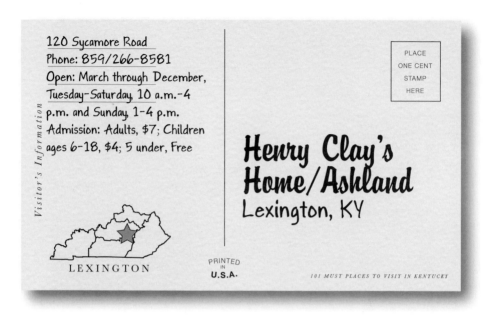

120 Sycamore Road

Phone: 859/266-8581

Open: March through December,

Tuesday–Saturday, 10 a.m.–4

p.m. and Sunday, 1–4 p.m.

Admission: Adults, $7; Children

ages 6–18, $4; 5 under, Free

Visitor's Information

PLACE
ONE CENT
STAMP
HERE

Henry Clay's Home/Ashland
Lexington, KY

LEXINGTON

PRINTED
IN
U.S.A.

101 MUST PLACES TO VISIT IN KENTUCKY

This National Historic Landmark, called Ashland, was the home to one of the nation's greatest statesmen, Henry Clay.

The beautiful two story brick home sits on 20 acres of land near downtown Lexington.

Clay, and his wife Lucretia, married in 1799, and by 1804 they began to acquire land for their new home "in the country."

The central section of the house was first built on the beautiful property that would soon grow to 600 acres, and because of the large number of majestic ash trees, Clay called his new home Ashland.

A few years later, new additions were added to each end of the

house giving it the majestic appearance it has today.

For some 40 years Henry Clay lived at Ashland, composing many of his eloquent speeches he delivered before the U.S. Congress.

The estate now includes the main house, several outbuildings and a beautiful formal garden.

Known as "The Great Compromiser," Clay died in 1852. He had been a major political force in the relatively early stages of government for close to 50 years. Growing up in Virginia he had been exposed to the American Revolution, having seen British troops ransack his family home when he was three-years old.

In 1803 he was first elected to the Kentucky General Assembly, and at the age of 29, Clay was appointed to the United States Senate. In 1808 he was chosen Speaker of the House of Representatives, and in 1810 he returned to the U.S. Senate. However, that same year he was once again elected to the House and served as speaker in the 12th, 13th, 14th, 15th and 16th Congresses.

Address and phone
numbers are listed below.

PLACE
ONE CENT
STAMP
HERE

Horse Farm Tours
Lexington Area

LEXINGTON

PRINTED
IN
U.S.A.

101 MUST PLACES TO VISIT IN KENTUCKY

What would living in Kentucky be without ever touring a Thoroughbred or Saddlebred horse farm?

One of the hallmarks of this state is the horse, and the Lexington area has more than 450 working Thoroughbred and Saddlebred farms. It is very important to know you should never drop by one of the farms unannounced.

Several of the horse farms offer tours by reservations only or through professional tour companies.

It is interesting to know that the American Saddlebred is the only horse breed to have originated in Kentucky. These are the horses that strut their stuff in show rings throughout the country. Shelbyville, in nearby Shelby County, is home to most of the Saddlebreds and prearranged tours can be scheduled by calling their tourism office at 502/633-6388.

Although some of the horse farms welcome prearranged visitors, they don't charge an admission. It, however, is customary to tip the farm representative showing you around.

184

Here are a few of the farms offering tours:

Clairborne Farms
859/987-2330
Near Paris, Ky
The great Secretariat is buried here.

Normandy Farm
859/294-9595
4701 Paris Pike.
*Home of the famous
L-shaped barn, replicated from a
barn in Normandy, France.*

Three Chimneys Farm
859/873-7053
Old Frankfort Pike in
Woodford County
Smarty Jones is here.

Ashford Stud
859/873-7088
In Woodford County
*Home to Derby winners Fusaichi
Pegasus and Thunder Gulch.*

Taylor Made Farm
859/885-3345
*The farm was origionally 120
acres, but is over 1,600 acres
today.*

Old Friends Farm
502/863-1775
Near Georgetown in Scott
County
*This farm is for retired
Thoroughbreds.*

Our Mims Retirement Haven
859/484-9582
In Paris, Ky
*This farm is for retired
Thoroughbred mares.*

Visitor's Information

4201 Versailles Road
Phone: 859/254-3412
Open: April and October
Admission: General $3
Call 1-800-456-3412 for
dining reservations

Keeneland Race Course
Lexington, KY

LEXINGTON

PRINTED
IN
U.S.A.

101 MUST PLACES TO VISIT IN KENTUCKY

Keeneland is one of those places you have to visit at least once even if thoroughbred horse racing is not your thing.

From the instant you turn onto the tree-lined driveway, there's a feeling of sophisticated elegance while at the same time not overdoing it.

Some of the structures are built of limestone quarried right there on the grounds in the early 1900s, and today the grounds and buildings take on a European look with their style and grace.

The one and 1/16th mile track was completed in 1936, and is now a National Historic Landmark. A little less commercialized than its sister track Churchill Downs in Louisville, Keeneland has made its own mark in the horse racing world. Visitors from all over come here to not only watch horses race during April and October, but also to train.

When the track first opened in 1936 there was seating enough for 2,500. But due to its success, capacity quickly rose to 5,000, and today the track can accommodate 25,000 spread out in the grandstands.

The track was named after Jack Keene, a prominent thoroughbred horse trainer, who began laying out the race course in 1916. Keene built a home and training complex on the grounds.

Keeneland's prominence among horse tracks makes this a must place to visit even if the horses aren't running at this 900 acre facility.

Keeneland began their horse sales back in the 1940s, in the beginning on a small scale. But today they have grown into the world's largest Thoroughbred auction, with over a half-billion dollars in gross annual sales.

You are encouraged to call for dates and times of races, sales and other events.

4089 Iron Works Parkway
Exit 120, I-75
800/678-8813 or
859/233-4303

Visitor's Information

Open: Daily from March 15–
October 31
Admission: $15/adult; $8/child
Wednesday–Sunday from
November 1–March 14
Admission: $9/adult; $6/child

PLACE
ONE CENT
STAMP
HERE

Kentucky Horse Park

Lexington, KY

LEXINGTON

PRINTED
IN
U.S.A.

101 MUST PLACES TO VISIT IN KENTUCKY

The Kentucky Horse Park is a year-round destination that has much to show and offer to young and old alike, and it's not just about the thoroughbred. It pays tribute to horses in general, hence the name Kentucky Horse Park.

The 1,200 acre attraction opened in 1978 after almost a decade of discussion about how to pay tribute to one of Kentucky's most recognizable commodities.

A portion of the park actually sits in Scott County on the Fayette County line just off I-75. Renowned horseman John Gaines is considered the brainchild of the park's establishment, that has hosted top horse people from throughout the world, including Princess Ann and Prince Philip. Well known horses such as Forego, standard bred legend Rambling Willie, John Henry and Cigar have called the Kentucky Horse Park home.

188

Today the park features over 50 different breeds of horses at work and play. Horse-drawn tours and carriage rides, horseback riding and pony rides allow visitors to actually have a "horse experience" on guided trail rides.

Two live shows are presented daily throughout the summer.

The International Museum of the Horse is the world's largest equestrian museum. Dedicated to all breeds of horses, the museum covers more than 50 million years of equine history, from the display of the earliest known ancestor of the horse to the impressive collection of trophies from famous Calumet Farm.

The Horse Park also has the American Saddle Bred Museum that displays exciting sights and sounds of the breed and its evolution into the modern-day horse.

The park has hosted some of the world's most prestigious equine events. One is the Rolex Kentucky, where Olympic challengers seek a spot on the U.S. Equestrian Team.

But in 2010 the crown jewel of equine events, the World Equestrian Championships, will come to Lexington.

833 West Main Street
Phone: 859/255-5522
Open: 8 a.m.-5 p.m. year-round

PLACE
ONE CENT
STAMP
HERE

Visitor's Information

Lexington Cemetery
Lexington, KY

LEXINGTON

PRINTED
IN
U.S.A.

101 MUST PLACES TO VISIT IN KENTUCKY

This beautiful cemetery, referred to by many as a "garden cemetery," was first opened in 1849 as Lexington's first rural cemetery.

Located at 833 West Main Street, the cemetery initially had 40 acres of land, but over the years has increased to its current 170 acres.

From the time visitors pass by the stately 1890 Romanesque-style gatehouse and into these peaceful grounds that contain an arboretum and dozens of varieties of trees, shrubs, plants and beautiful flowers, they will recognize that this is special.

Two large lakes in the cemetery are pleasing to the eye, and also provide a habitat for ducks, swans and other birds attracted to the water features.

The Lexington Cemetery is the final resting place for many well-known Kentuckians.

A magnificent monument in tribute to Kentucky's famous senator and three time presidential candidate, Henry Clay. He served as a United States Senator and Representative from Kentucky.

The cemetery also incorporates one of eight national cemeteries in Kentucky and contains the remains of Union, Confederate and Spanish-American War veterans.

It is also noted in the cemetery that back in 1775 several backwoodsmen first set their sites on what would become Lexington.

Other famous people buried here are John C. Breckinridge, Vice-President of the United States under James Buchanan, author James Lane Allen, Confederate soldier John Hunt Morgan, basketball coach Adolph Rupp, and actor Jim Varney.

Located at Kentucky Horse Park
4089 Iron Works Parkway
Phone: 859/233-4303 or
800/878-8813

Visitor's Information

PLACE
ONE CENT
STAMP
HERE

Man O'War's Grave
Lexington, KY

LEXINGTON

PRINTED
IN
U.S.A.

101 MUST PLACES TO VISIT IN KENTUCKY

Some say Man O'War was the greatest thoroughbred race horse ever. There have been others, and surely there will be more, but this horse will stack his record up against them all.

It was Man O'War, however, who struck a chord at a time when our nation was looking for something good to cling to.

There were sports heroes out there. Babe Ruth among them, but it was this horse who held his own. Obviously Man O'War couldn't talk the talk, others did that for him. But he definitely walked the walk, and most certainly ran the race.

Think about this. Twenty one starts, twenty wins. The great one's only loss was to a horse appropriately named Upset.

When Man O'War died in November 1947 it was major national news. Gone was the horse that would set the standard by which all future racing thoroughbreds would be measured. It was only appropriate that the horse be buried in the style in which he raced. First class.

Man O'War was embalmed and lay in state for several days in a-first-of-its-kind casket lined with his racing colors. It was reported that more than 2,000 people attended his funeral.

After initially being buried at Faraway Farm Memorial Park on Hoffman Hill Pike by owner Samuel Riddle, Man O'War was later moved to the Kentucky Horse Park.

The move did not come without some public controversy, as many felt Man O'War should remain where originally buried. The great horse was born in 1917 and lived for a little more than 30 years.

Today a full-size statue of the horse adorns the grave site surrounded by the burial grounds for sons War Admiral and War Relic.

I don't know who votes on things like this, I know I never have, but whoever does, they got this one right.

Voted one of the 10 best scenic drives in the United States, this almost-17 miles, two-lane drive, is over much too soon. You may want to turn around and drive it again and again. Who would blame you?

Of course the trail can begin or end from either Frankfort, Kentucky's state capital, or Lexington. It matters not about the posted speed limit, because it's a sure bet you will be driving real slow.

On one end the drive begins just past the intersection of New Circle Road in Lexington and travels into Franklin County to Old Frankfort Pike where it connects with U.S. 60.

The drive will take you past beautiful thoroughbred horse farms in a postcard-like setting. Hand-stacked rock walls, historic old buildings, that include a wonderful little eatery regularly frequented by horse farm people, add to the ambience of the trek.

Trees, lots of them, border the route. Depend-

194

ing on when you visit, the dogwoods and redbuds can be described as spectacular in the spring. When the oaks, maples, locusts and osage oranges are in full leaf, much of the scenic byway is in the shade of their huge canopies that suspend over the roadway.

Behind miles and miles of black and white plank fencing, thoroughbreds can be seen grazing on Kentucky bluegrass. Among the noted horse farms are Darby Dan, Donamire, Old Frankfort Stud, Buckrom Oak, and Three Chimneys. And if Three Chimneys rings a bell it might be because it is the home of Smarty Jones, the 2004 Kentucky Derby winner, and Big Brown the 2008 Derby champion.

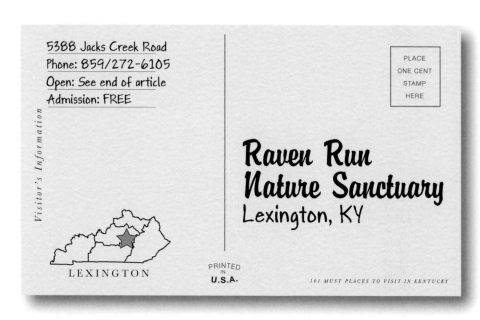

5388 Jacks Creek Road
Phone: 859/272-6105
Open: See end of article
Admission: FREE

PLACE
ONE CENT
STAMP
HERE

Raven Run
Nature Sanctuary
Lexington, KY

LEXINGTON

PRINTED
IN
U.S.A.

101 MUST PLACES TO VISIT IN KENTUCKY

By nature park standards this 470-acre sanctuary might be considered small. But that doesn't mean it's not worth visiting.

With over 10 miles of trails and a nature center for observation and education, this park offers quite a few historic and geologic points of interest. Over 600 species of plants, 200 species of birds, and 57 species of butterflies have been charted here.

This southern Fayette County venue allows visitors a wooded walk to an overlook on the Kentucky River, and then down into a scenic creek gorge. The name, Raven Run, comes from the name of the creek that meanders through the area before emptying into the Kentucky River.

Originally the area was settled and farmed over 200 years ago. A house built there in the late 1700s on a Revolutionary War land grant still stands.

The well-developed trails

system features what is called the Red Trail. It's the longest and runs in a counterclockwise loop that permits hikers to traverse up to a 100-foot bluff overlooking the Kentucky River, and then descends into the Raven Run gorge to an old 19th century gristmill.

Everyone who visits Raven Run must first sign in at the nature center, which is located at the beginning of the trailhead. An added bonus is all of the unique displays, several hands-on exhibits, and lots of pamphlets about birds, mammals and ferns.

A caution to visitors who plan to hike: bring a water container. Although water is available at the sanctuary there are no fountains at the nature center or on the trails.

Open: January, February, November, December, 9 a.m.–5 p.m., daily
March and October, Monday through Thursday, 9 a.m.–5 p.m.
Friday, Saturday & Sunday, 9 a.m.–6 p.m.
April and May, Monday through Thursday, 9 a.m.–5 p.m.
Friday, Saturday and Sunday, 9 a.m.-7 p.m.
June and July, Monday through Thursday, 9 a.m.–5 p.m.
Friday, Saturday and Sunday, 9 a.m.–8 p.m.
August and September, Monday through Thursday, 9 a.m.–5 p.m.

Berea, Kentucky	Berea, Ky
Breaks Interstate Park	Pike County, Ky
Carter Caves	Olive Hill, Ky
Country Music Highway	Eastern Kentucky
Cumberland Falls	Corbin, Ky
Cumberland Gap	Middlesboro, Ky
Harland Sanders Café	Corbin, Ky
Hillbilly Days	Pikeville, Ky
Mountain Arts Center	Prestonsburg, Ky
Natural Bridge	Slade, Ky
Pikeville Cut-Through	Pikeville, Ky
Red River Gorge	Slade, Ky
Stearns, Kentucky	Stearns, Ky
World Chicken Festival	London, Ky

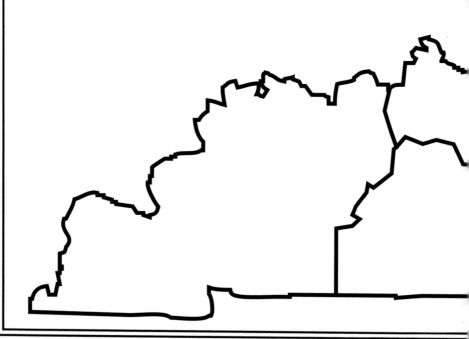

Eastern Region

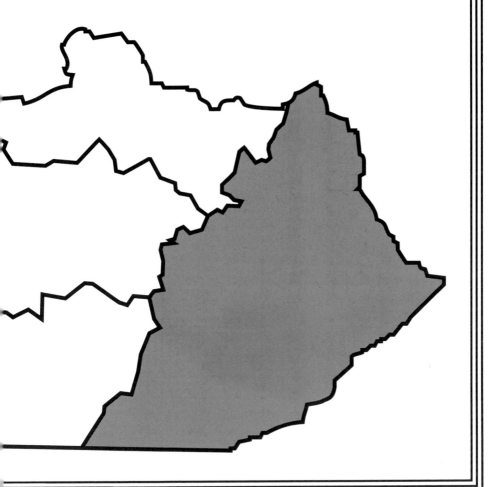

I-75, Exits 76 & 77
Phone: 800/598-5263
Boone Tavern: 800/366-9358
Kentucky Artisan Center:
859/985-5448

Visitor's Information

EASTERN

PRINTED
IN
U.S.A.

Berea, KY

101 MUST PLACES TO VISIT IN KENTUCKY

Most people, when they think of Berea, also think of Boone Tavern and the college.

The charming small town is so intertwined with production of world-class crafts and recently renovated Boone Tavern that they are almost impossible to separate.

Berea College is unique in that it offers four years of free tuition as a trade-out for on-campus work that includes the Tavern, which the college oversees.

The more than 155-year-old college has produced hand-crafted products by students and residents of the Appalachians, and because of the quality, Berea has made it a major focus in drawing tourists.

Believe it or not Boone Tavern started out as a guest house for the college when it opened in 1909. Named

after Kentucky legendary explorer, Daniel Boone, the 58-room hotel became known for handcrafted furniture in the rooms and friendly college students staffing much of the day-to-day operation.

Boone Tavern is also synonymous with good food. And here it starts with their signature spoon bread. The menu is heavy with dishes of southern cuisine. Either before or after dinner, visitors like to get a little seat time in the oversized rocking chairs that are a staple of the beautiful exterior porch.

Anyone who visits Berea will want to explore the entire area, because there are numerous shops scattered everywhere.

Shops and galleries are in close proximity to Boone Tavern, and in the Old Town district there are some 40 galleries, studios and antique shops. At the edge of Berea sits the Kentucky Artisan Center just off of I-75 at Exit 77. Operated by the state, it is destination in itself.

Berea was recognized several years ago by the state legislature as the Folk Arts & Crafts Capital of Kentucky, and if you've already been there you know why. If you haven't you'll see why.

Pikeville Tourism Office
800/844-7453

PLACE
ONE CENT
STAMP
HERE

Visitor's Information

Breaks Interstate Park
Pike County, KY

EASTERN

PRINTED
IN
U.S.A.

101 MUST PLACES TO VISIT IN KENTUCKY

Perhaps the least known of Kentucky's State Parks, the Breaks Interstate Park sits in both Pike County, Kentucky and Dickerson County, Virginia. It's one of those odd arrangements that dates back to 1954 when the two states got together and decided they had something special that needed to be developed so people could come and see.

Often described as the Grand Canyon of the South, this 4,500 acre park is made up of deep green woodlands, sky-scraping mountain scenery, deep creviced gorges, unusual rock formations, numerous hidden springs, and an abundance of strategically placed overlooks for visitors to enjoy.

With all of this said, not many Kentuckians are even aware of the Breaks or where it is located.

In Virginia, the Breaks ranks among the top five state parks, with visitation exceeding 350,000. What makes this joint venture a little different is that although much of the park is in Kentucky, the state receives no actual rev-

enue from the lodge, cabins, campgrounds and restaurants that are actually in Virginia.

It was a Kentuckian, over 50 years ago, who pushed for the park.

Pikeville businessman, Kelly Day, pushed the initiative that led Kentucky Governor Lawrence Whetherby and Virginia's Governor to enact an agreement.

The Breaks Park offers the Rhododendron Lodge, an 82-room facility with a restaurant that serves up an incredible view.

For the most part, many of the Park's activities shut down the week before Christmas, and don't re-open until April. The two-bedroom, fully equipped cottages, however, are open year-round.

Russell Fork on the Big Sandy River has become quite popular for white water rafting. Much depends on scheduled water releases from the nearby reservoir. Usually water is released on Saturdays and Sundays in October. Call ahead for river activities.

Not the easiest place to reach, the Interstate Breaks Park, is a little over 30 miles from Pikeville. Take Hwy. 80 to Elkhorn City, and then you are another twisting-turning-meet-yourself seven miles to the park.

It's worth it!

Carter Caves touts some 20 caves within the boundaries of this State Park Resort in Carter County.

The park, first established in 1946 after a group of local citizens stepped up and donated some land to the state, gives Kentucky two areas of the state that visitors can enjoy a cave experience.

Usually getting most of the cave attention has been the Mammoth Cave area of South Central Kentucky, but Carter Caves has a series of caverns it, too, can be proud of.

The most popular cave in the Carter Cave group is X Cave, so named because of two intersecting caverns that form an X. Filled with stalactites and stalagmites, this beautiful show cave boasts incredible formations churned out by both the passing of water and time. A trek through X Cave will consist of narrow as well as tall passageways.

During the winter months an estimated 40,000 Indiana bats hibernate in, you guessed it, Bat Cave. The bats pose no threat to visitors, but still the cave is closed during winter months for the bat's protection.

The largest cave in the park is Cascade Cave. It also features beautiful formations that include a 30-foot high underground waterfall. This cave also has a reflecting pool, cathedral room, and even an area where dances were held years ago.

A number of other caves are open for tours with some being self guided.

Carter Caves State Resort Park also features a 28-room lodge with a 100-seat restaurant. Cottages and campsites are also available.

Visitor's Information

Country Music Highway
Eastern Kentucky

EASTERN

PRINTED
IN
U.S.A.

101 MUST PLACES TO VISIT IN KENTUCKY

T his 118 mile trek along U.S. 23 is something special for those who enjoy scenic venues, challenging golf courses, lively entertainment, a handful of state parks, and some very interesting shopping.

Created to pay tribute to the major country major stars from the mountains of eastern Kentucky this collection of small towns offers up a little something for everyone. It's definitely a getaway that you will want to allow two or three days for in order to see it all.

Greenup to the north, all the way to Jenkins to the south, and all points in between showcase the talented singers that over the years worked their way to the top, becoming some of the most recognizable names in the entertainment business. And yes, even the Grand Ole Opry!

Billy Ray Cyrus (Flat-

206

woods), Wynona and Naomi Judd (Ashland), Tom T. Hall (Olive Hill), Keith Whitley (Sandy Hook), Ricky Skaggs (Cordell), Larry Cordle (Cordell), Loretta Lynn (Paintsville), Crystal Gayle (Paintsville), HyLo Brown (Paintsville), Dwight Yoakum (Prestonsburg), Patty Loveless (Pikeville), and Gary Stewart (Whitesburg), are some of the more prominent names along U.S. 23.

In Paintsville visitors can stop in at the U.S. 23 Country Music Highway Museum where they can see in detail what all of these local stars have contributed to the music culture of the region. By all means stop in at Loretta Lynn's old home place in Butcher Hollow.

Although country music is the hook to draw visitors, it's a promise that there's enough things to see and do that will make you want to come back to see the rest of it.

Venues like the Paramount Arts Center in Ashland, Carter Caves State Park in Olive Hill, Greenbo Lake State Park in Greenup, Mountain Home Place in Staffordville, Breaks Interstate Park near Pikeville, Kentucky Opry and Jenny Wiley Theater in Prestonsburg are just a few of the other attractions visitors will want to take in.

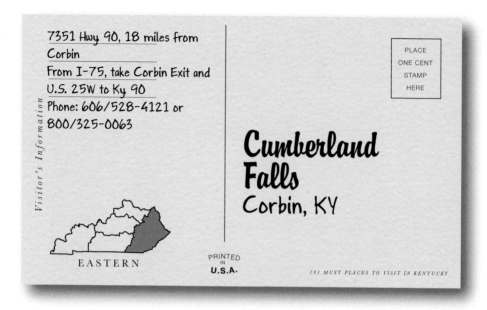

7351 Hwy 90, 18 miles from Corbin

From I-75, take Corbin Exit and U.S. 25W to Ky 90

Phone: 606/528-4121 or 800/325-0063

Visitor's Information

Cumberland Falls
Corbin, KY

EASTERN

PRINTED
IN
U.S.A.

101 MUST PLACES TO VISIT IN KENTUCKY

In Kentucky the Cumberland Falls is known as the "Niagara of the South." It's easy to see why.

There's something about a waterfall that brings excitement and wonder, especially when the falls is 125-feet wide and cascades some 60-feet below onto huge boulders that creates a mist of water that dampens those visitors who take a boat tour below the falls.

Regardless of the time of year, a trip to see Cumberland Falls is well worth it. At the falls there is occasionally an added attraction, and it happens at night – depending on the weather.

It's referred to as "the magical moon bow." It's only visible on a clear night under a full moon. The moon bow is a phenomenon not found anywhere else in the Western Hemisphere. The only other site in the world is reported to be Victoria Falls in Africa.

The weather has to be just right, but believe it or not it happens quite often.

When you see the moon bow you'll know it. Created by the light from a full moon shining through the water's spray that acts as tiny prisms, a whitish color appears. Some even say they can see different colors projecting from the falls.

Nothing is for certain on viewing a moon bow, however, some times throughout the year seem to be better than others. Call ahead for these dates.

Cumberland Falls is part of Cumberland Falls State Resort Park. An impressive old 1941 lodge offers up 51 overnight rooms as well as the availability of several cabins. The lodge also has an ample dining facility.

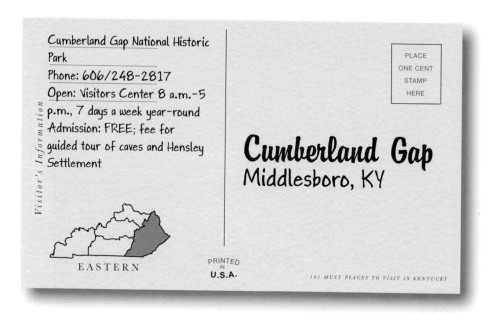

Cumberland Gap National Historic
Park

Phone: 606/248-2817

Open: Visitors Center 8 a.m.–5
p.m., 7 days a week year-round

Admission: FREE; fee for
guided tour of caves and Hensley
Settlement

PLACE
ONE CENT
STAMP
HERE

Cumberland Gap
Middlesboro, KY

EASTERN

PRINTED
IN
U.S.A.

101 MUST PLACES TO VISIT IN KENTUCKY

Contrary to popular legend, Daniel Boone did not discover Cumberland Gap. Instead it was Dr. Thomas Walker, a Virginia physician who became an adventurer. It was in 1750 when he discovered the small gap in the Cumberland Mountains that would eventually lead hunters into Kentucky's fertile hunting grounds.

In his lifetime, Boone passed through the Gap many times, and by the time Kentucky became the fifteenth state in 1792, more than 100,000 people had passed through Cumberland Gap.

In 1775, Daniel Boone, history says, was hired to widen the gap in order to make it easier to reach Kentucky. And then, later, in 1796, it was widened again to allow for wagon travel.

The scene at Cumberland Gap today doesn't resemble what our forefathers saw over 250 years ago.

The Cumberland Gap uniquely sits near where the state line of Kentucky, Tennessee and Virginia meet.

In 1996, at a cost of $280 million, a four-lane twin-bore mountain tunnel was opened. The 4,600-foot long highway that travels beneath the Gap carries 18,000 cars and trucks of Kentucky-Tennessee traffic daily on U.S. Hwy. 25-E.

Once the sixteen year tunnel project was completed, efforts were then turned to restore the original Cumberland Gap trail that visitors can see today.

A visitors center interprets how and why Cumberland Gap was the first great gateway to the West, following a pathway first created by the buffalo, Native Americans, the long hunters, and then the settlers.

Self-guided and ranger-led tours are available in order to get a closer view of lush forest, cascading waterfalls and beautiful scenery.

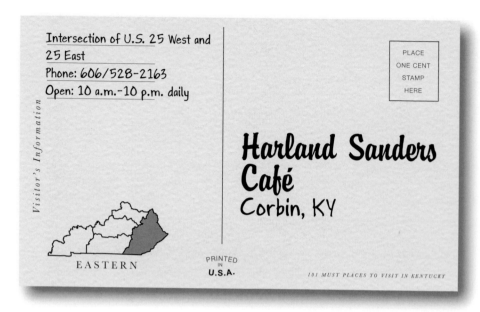

Intersection of U.S. 25 West and
25 East
Phone: 606/528-2163
Open: 10 a.m.–10 p.m. daily

Visitor's Information

Harland Sanders Café
Corbin, KY

EASTERN

PRINTED
IN
U.S.A.

101 MUST PLACES TO VISIT IN KENTUCKY

The birthplace of Kentucky Fried Chicken where Harland Sanders started it all has to be a "must places to visit" in Kentucky.

It's a historical site. . .at least in Kentucky.

This museum-like building has a KFC sign out front indicating that it is a chain restaurant, but for sure it's unlike any KFC you've been in before.

It once served as a restaurant and motel on U.S. 25 in the 1940s, and it was another Kentuckian, Duncan Hines from Bowling Green,

who helped the Colonel get started when he listed the Corbin restaurant in his 1939 travel guide as a "good place to eat."

The restaurant has been restored even to the point of exhibits depicting the original kitchen, and another showing what one of the motel rooms was like.

A multitude of tributes to the Colonel fill the walls pertaining to his life and travels throughout the world.

Of all of the great food franchises across the country, this is the only one that still operates as a restaurant.

"The original McDonald's and the very first Pizza Hut are no longer restaurants," says owner John R. Neal. "But our restaurant here is still going strong and one of the tops in the country."

Harland Sanders Café is a big bite of Americana and Neal says the restaurant stands today restored and preserved as a landmark in the history of American commerce.

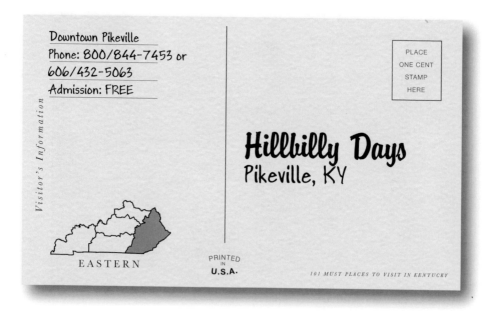

Visitor's Information

Downtown Pikeville
Phone: 800/844-7453 or
606/432-5063
Admission: FREE

PLACE
ONE CENT
STAMP
HERE

Hillbilly Days
Pikeville, KY

EASTERN

PRINTED
IN
U.S.A.

101 MUST PLACES TO VISIT IN KENTUCKY

Hillbilly Days is a three-day event that draws some 100,000 visitors each April to Pikeville.

One of the things that make this event that started in 1977 so special is that it is a fundraiser to benefit the Shriners Children's Hospital in Lexington several hours away.

This Thursday-Friday-Saturday festival draws visitors from throughout several states and literally has something fun and entertaining for an

entire family. With this many people it's easy to see why the entire down-town portion of Pikeville is blocked off to traffic.

Bands mean music, and music means people dancing and singing. Major arts and crafts vendors, food, food and more food, only at Hill-billy Days it's referred to as vittles. One of the marquee events is the quilt show, and what would a Shriners event be without a Main Street parade? You may never see such a wild assortment of cars, limousines, pick-up trucks and scooters.

Other happenings are a cash prizes-corn hole tournament, 5-mile road race and fun run for kids.

A festival of this magnitude has to have a carnival midway. Merry-Go-Rounds, Ferris Wheel, Spook House, it's all here.

Facilities are available for campers and motor homes, and it's prob-ably a good idea to book lodging reservations in advance.

While in Pike County you can also enjoy visiting the scenic Pikeville Cut-Through Project, and the beautiful Breaks Interstate Park. Both of these are also featured in this book. And what would a visit to the area be without seeing some of the Hatfield-McCoy Feud sites?

The Country Music Highway on U.S. 23 in eastern Kentucky winds and twists its way, passing through, by or near, where many of the biggest names to ever sing a song were either born or grew up.

So it is only fitting that the Mountain Arts Center in Prestonsburg is located in the proximity of these legendary names.

The MAC, as it is called, is a 3,050 seat theater that draws visitors from a five-state area. The state-of-art venue opened in 1996, and since then has gained a reputation of bringing not just the so-called biggies, but also providing a forum for incredible mountain talent.

Over the years names like Dwight Yoakum, Loretta Lynn, Billy Ray Cyrus, George Jones, Montgomery Gentry, Ricky Skaggs, Patty Loveless and Merle Haggard are just a few of the country music stars to have spent some time on the MAC stage.

The MAC has also played host to some of the biggest names in gospel music as well as family theater productions like *Annie, The King and*

I, On Golden Pond and *Always Patsy Cline*.

To further point out the versatility of this fantastic facility, the Tommy Dorsey and Glenn Miller Orchestras have performed here.

There is always something going on at the MAC.

Regardless of who the headlines acts are that perform here, visitors seem to come away talking about the locals that entertain. The MAC is home to Billie Jean Osborne's Kentucky Opry and the Kentucky Opry Jr. Pros. This is the resident performing group at the Center. And perform they do. Their musical variety presentation is a fast-paced performance that includes a sizzling set of country, bluegrass, oldies, gospel and patriotic favorites.

You won't be disappointed.

217

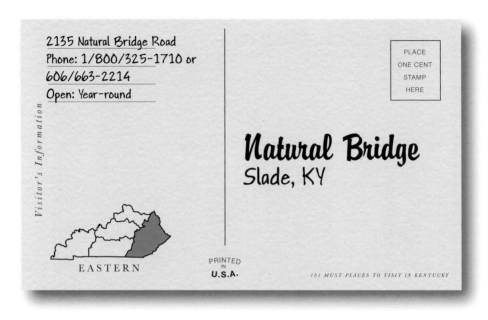

2135 Natural Bridge Road
Phone: 1/800/325-1710 or
606/663-2214
Open: Year-round

Visitor's Information

Natural Bridge
Slade, KY

EASTERN

PRINTED
IN
U.S.A.

101 MUST PLACES TO VISIT IN KENTUCKY

Formed over millions of years by Mother Nature, this great natural sandstone arch is located in the middle of Daniel Boone National Forest at Natural Bridge State Park in eastern Kentucky.

Today it is all a part of a nature preserve system consisting of over 1,100 acres.

Although the huge arch, which takes on the appearance of a bridge, is the focal point of the terrain, there are literally hundreds of natural arches and bridges within the area.

There is really no bad time to visit Natural Bridge, but some hiking veterans say they prefer the winter because less foliage opens up lots of spectacular viewing sheds not normally seen.

This Powell County attraction was dedicated as a State Park and nature preserve in 1981, and now includes a 35 room lodge tucked into a beautiful mountainside that visitors can view from their rooms private balconies. There are also

218

10 cottages that range from efficiency to one and two bedrooms. A full service dining room is in the lodge.

For those interested, there are 13 miles of hiking trails over what is considered moderate to strenuous. These trails, which can be guided, include trekking along rugged cliffs and past rock shelters. When hiking in unfamiliar surrounding, you are cautioned to be aware of the dangers of this rugged area.

The lodge has the amenities of meeting rooms and swimming pool. Two park campgrounds offer 82 sites.

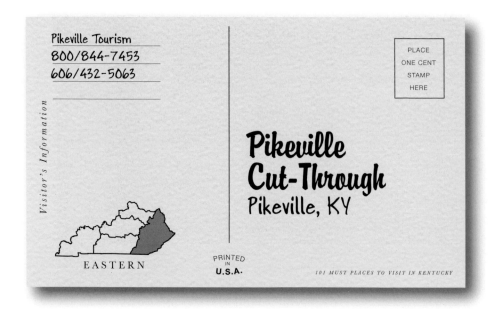

Pikeville Cut-Through
Pikeville, KY

I
t's the town that moved a mountain – literally.

For decades the small town of Pikeville in eastern Kentucky dreaded to see the spring rains come to the mountains. It usually meant the overflowing of the Levisa Fork of the Big Sandy River as it meandered its way through the downtown area.

All the while the railroad also ran through the middle of town, and the coal dust from the railcars heading north resulted in buildings and streets constantly being covered.

The locations of the river and railroad had become a heavy burden to overcome in future economic development and quality of life for Pikeville and its residents.

Enter Dr. William C. Hambley.

He had grown up in Pikeville and seen the ravage of the almost annual floods, and the congestion caused by the railroad and three major roads converging in the downtown area. After receiving his medical degree, he returned home in 1954 with a vision.

His vision included relocating the railroad tracks and rerouting the river. It was almost laughable to some, but not to those Dr. Hambley had convinced it could work.

After being elected mayor in 1960, Dr. Hambley set about to work his plan, and 13 years later the first phase of his almost unthinkable goal of moving the railroad and river was underway.

The Pikeville Cut-Through project became one of the largest engineering and earthmoving accomplishments ever in this western hemisphere, second only to the Panama Canal. The Cut-Through was 1,300 feet wide, 3,700 feet long and 523 feet deep.

After beginning in 1973 and being completed in 1987, the 14 year endeavor had not only "saved the town," but created over 390 downtown acres that allowed Pikeville to be reborn. Structures, housing government, recreation, entertainment, commercial, and medical facilities have come to life, and Pikeville is now one of the anchors of eastern Kentucky.

Twelve million cubic yards of rock and dirt were moved in order to bring Dr. Hambley's vision to reality, and today an overlook pad is there for visitors to view the "new" Pikeville and see the enormity of what was involved in moving a mountain.

Natural Bridge State Resort Park,
800/325-1710
Red River Outdoors,
606/663-9701

PLACE
ONE CENT
STAMP
HERE

Visitor's Information

Red River Gorge
Slade, KY

EASTERN

PRINTED
IN
U.S.A.

101 MUST PLACES TO VISIT IN KENTUCKY

Rock climbers from throughout the United States have visited the Red River Gorge to test their skills in this geological wonder located just off the Bert Combs Mountain Parkway near Slade, Kentucky.

The 26,000-acre area is in both the Daniel Boone National Forest and the Natural Bridge State Park. The raw beauty of leafless trees with sandstone cliffs as a backdrop make it a stunning place to visit even in winter or early spring. Random sized icicles can often be seen still dripping, offering up a scene and the feel of looking into a fantasy land.

Even though Red River Gorge attracts serious rock climbers, it also has a soft spot for hikers. There's a trail to accommodate almost any level of hiking. A word of caution: follow the rules and signs. Those who wander off marked trails risk coming upon cliffs very suddenly. Closely supervise children, and don't walk beneath the icicles. They sometimes fall.

If an encounter with a rocky cliff or winding hiking trail is not for you, perhaps the 30-mile automobile ride will allow you to see this natural wonder in a less strenuous manner.

To get started from the Mountain Parkway, travel to Slade at Exit 33. There you begin the loop at the junction of Kentucky Highway 11 and 15. Several of the roads are narrow and winding, but remember you're not going to be in a hurry anyway. By all means you'll want to allow enough time to pull over and take short walks, marked by signage, to some of the most scenic views of natural rock formations anywhere in the world.

There's also another way you can experience Red River Gorge. There are Class II and Class III rapids on the river and they can be dangerous. A limited number of outfitters are in the area, and it is recommended you do your homework and learn the lay of the land before undertaking a river float.

Red River Gorge is one of the nation's most spectacular natural wonders and it's right here in Kentucky. Many of the area businesses and convenience stores have handy maps available.

McCreary County Tourism
888/284-3718

Visitor's Information

Stearns, KY

PLACE
ONE CENT
STAMP
HERE

EASTERN

PRINTED
IN
U.S.A.

101 MUST PLACES TO VISIT IN KENTUCKY

S tearns and nearby Whitley City sit near the Tennessee-Kentucky border in Southeastern Kentucky. Both are surrounded by the southern portion of the Daniel Boone National Forest and northern section of the Big South Fork National River and Recreational Area.

The country is beautifully rugged, as once were the people who worked there years ago. Today the area is placing much of its future in the people who visit the area and realize their efforts to get there were worthwhile.

There is something to see and do for all ages.

But first a little history.

In 1902, Justus Stearns, living in Michigan, bought 30,000 acres of timberland in this part of Kentucky. But soon after, coal was discovered on the property and shortly the Stearns Coal & Lumber Company was established.

The company built the town of Stearns to serve as the center of the mining and logging business that controlled some 200 square miles of land. The Stearns Company also built the Kentucky-Tennessee Railroad, and opened the first all-electric sawmill in the United States, all while employing over 2,200 people living and working in 18 coal and lumber camps.

In the 1950s the Stearns economic situation took a downward turn. Mines were closed, and by 1976 Stearns had been sold to Blue Diamond Coal, who then transferred its vast holdings to the National Forest, Big

224

South Fork, and private ownership. The last mine closed in 1987.

The coal camps were closed, eventually leaving only the stories of the miners and their families, and the beauty of the natural surroundings behind.

A footnote to the Stearns legacy is that Justus Stearns had built a nine-hole golf course which is the second oldest course in Kentucky. Today it is the Stearns Golf Course.

The featured attraction today is the Big South Fork Scenic Railway, a 16-mile train ride through a thick forested gorge, with a creek on one side and a steep cliff on the other. Travelers can choose to sit in glass-enclosed or open cars, usually depending on the weather.

Barthell Coal Camp is very interesting, and although the train doesn't stop there, it is well worth a visit on your own. Visitors can overnight here as well as tour a mine.

The train does stop at the Blue Heron Coal Camp for self-guided tours that include a coal tipple.

While in Stearns, be sure to visit the Sweet Kreations Gift Shoppe located in the Depot.

Phone: 800/348-0095
Website: www.chickenfestival.com

Visitor's Information

World Chicken Festival
London, KY

EASTERN

PRINTED
IN
U.S.A.

101 MUST PLACES TO VISIT IN KENTUCKY

Mark your calendar for the last full weekend of September because the World Chicken Festival is something you've got to visit at least once.

The four-day event routinely attracts some 250,000 visitors each year to eat chicken, enjoy the entertainment, or ride some rides on the carnival's midway. As you can imagine, several blocks of London's downtown are blocked off to make room for the throngs of people. Many come to see the parade, while others come to enter the cooking contest. But, make no mistake about it, almost everyone stops by to see the world's largest skillet.

And what a skillet it is!

Since 1992, this giant skillet has cooked well over 40,000 dinners. It weighs 700 pounds, 10-feet, six inches in diameter, eight inches deep, and sports an eight foot handle.

But that's not all!

To cook the 8,000 pieces of chicken, it requires 375 pounds of

flour, 75 pounds of salt, 30 pounds each of pepper and paprika, and, of course, World Chicken Festival's special ingredients.

Natural gas is the fuel source for frying the chicken, and some 60 gallons are used in order to cook at 325-350 degrees. This amount of gas is more than an average family would use in a year.

Laurel County has a spectacular history with chicken, and in case you haven't figured it out by now, this is where Col. Harland Sanders started peddling his product, in nearby Corbin back in the 1940s. In fact, his first restaurant is part of the World Chicken Festival doings, in that the public is encouraged to make the trek to see the restaurant that has been turned into a museum and is listed in this book.

A footnote to it all is that another well-known chicken eatery also got its start in Laurel County. Lee Cummings, along with his uncle, opened the first Lee's Famous Recipe back in 1952.

About the Author

Gary P. West grew up in Elizabeth-town, Kentucky and attended Western Kentucky University before graduating from the University of Kentucky with a degree in journalism in 1967.

At UK he was a daily sports editor for the *Kentucky Kernel*.

Later he served as editor for the nation's largest civilian enterprise military newspaper at Fort Bragg, North Carolina. From there he went to work as an advertising copywriter in the corporate office of one the country's largest insurance companies, State Farm Insurance in Bloomington, Illinois.

In 1972 he returned to Kentucky where he began publishing an advertising shopper in Bowling Green.

Along the way, for twelve years, he worked in the athletic department as executive director of the Hilltopper Athletic Foundation at Western Kentucky University, and provided color commentary on the Hilltopper Basketball Network.

In 1993 he became executive director of the Bowling Green Area Convention and Visitors Bureau, where he solidified his background in hospitality. He is a freelance writer for several magazines, in addition to writing a syndicated newspaper column, *Out & About... Kentucky Style*, for a number of papers across the state.

In 2005 he wrote the highly acclaimed biography, *King Kelly Coleman–Kentucky's Greatest Basketball Legend*, in 2006, the best selling travel guide *Eating Your Way Across Kentucky*, and in 2007, its sequel *Eating Your Way Across Kentucky-The Recipes*, and in 2008, *Shopping Your Way Across Kentucky*.

Photo Credits

Dollhouse Museum/Danville
Credit: Ann Dudley McCall (outside photo)

Cumberland Gap/Middlesboro
Credit: Cumberland Gap National Park

Bill Monroe Home/Rosine
Credit: Mike Morbeck (jamming photo)

Breaks Interstate Park/Pikeville
Credit: Kentucky Tourism

Bourbon Trail
Credit: Kentucky Tourism

State Capital/Frankfort
Credit: Kentucky Tourism

Carter Cave/Olive Hill
Credit: Kentucky Tourism

Churchill Downs/Louisville
Credit: Kentucky Tourism

Columbus-Belmont Park/Columbus
Credit: Kentucky Tourism

Cumberland Falls/Corbin
Credit: Kentucky Tourism

Frankfort Cemetery/Frankfort
Credit: Kentucky Tourism (Daniel Boone
Monument only)
Credit: Gene Burch

Center for Kentucky History/Frankfort
Credit: Kentucky Tourism

Gov. Mansion/Frankfort
Credit: Kentucky Tourism (exterior photo)
Credit: Gene Burch (interior only)

Horse Farm Tour/Lexington
Credit: Kentucky Tourism

Kentucky Horse Park/Lexington
Credit: Kentucky Tourism
Credit: Marc Manning (Man O War)

Man O'War/Lexington
Credit: Kentucky Tourism

Federal Hill/Bardstown
Credit: Kentucky Tourism

Natural Bridge
Credit: Kentucky Tourism

Old Frankfort Pike/Lexington
Credit: Kentucky Tourism

Old State Capitol/Frankfort
Credit: Kentucky Tourism (exterior photo)
Credit: Gene Burch (interior only)

Red River Gorge/Slade
Credit: Kentucky Tourism

Shaker Village/Harrodsburg
Credit: Kentucky Tourism

Wine Tour
Credit: Kentucky Tourism

Raven Run/Lexington
Credit: C. Michael Downs

Louisville Slugger Museum/Louisville
Credit: Louisville Slugger Museum & Factory

Bernheim Arboretum/Shepherdsville
Credit: Bernheim Arboretum and Research
Forest

National Corvette Museum/Bowling Green
Credit: Dan Bowman (inside photo only)

Trinity-St. X Football/Louisville
Credit: F. Scott Scinta (line of scrimmage)
Credit: James Dawson (coin toss)

Falls of the Ohio/Louisville
Credit: Garrick Fields

Covered Bridges/Kentucky
Credit: Kentucky Tourism

Index

231